Protecting Cancer Patients: controlling risk factors, restraining cost of drugs and preventing financial catastrophe

R.N. Bhardwaj Ph.D.
Professor of Economics
George Brown College (Toronto)

&

Contributor: Atul Bhardwaj
Free Lance Data Scientist

Executive Summary

Cancer has become a major public health challenge in countries at all income levels. Despite impressive advancements in biomedical research, improved understanding of relevant risk factors and increased survival rates in developed nations, the rising incidence rate (new cases) of cancer is, however, becoming a formidable challenge. The growing burden of cancer illness is projected to increase for several decades due to demographic and epidemiological transitions already ongoing in low- and middle-income countries (LMICs). In addition to the disease burden, patients, caregivers, third party payers (insurance companies and public health authorities), and physicians are also met with the worrisome challenge of rapidly increasing costs of new cancer drugs.

Escalating prices of cancer drugs have evoked concern among stakeholders about the financial burden faced by patients in accessing life-saving treatment. There is now a general consensus that the current model of drug development needs thorough streamlining. Cost-containment strategy calls for addressing the issue of declining R&D productivity trends and reforming the drugs pricing system. Regarding the productivity puzzle, the present study has analyzed both the efficiency and effectiveness aspects of the drug discovery and development process. New suggested approaches for improving efficiency are presented in this document. These include, matching drugs to the patient's molecular profile, "adaptive trial" designs (i.e., using interim analysis to customize the trials), alternative surrogate endpoints, expedited regulatory review procedures, new open models of collaboration, multidisciplinary research on a global scale, and applications of computational biology and bioinformatics advancements. The proposed value-based pricing approach is also reviewed in this study as a means of achieving cost effectiveness.

Patient advocacy group, expressing concerns, have alleged that pharmaceutical companies are using their monopoly power in setting the prices of new anticancer agents. Contemporary pharmaceutical industry pricing practices lack transparency on the company's R&D expenditure data. Soaring prices along with inadequate public funding programs in many countries for catastrophic drug coverage are resulting in an alarming proportion of out-of-pocket (OOP) expenses on life-saving drugs. The majority of the population in LMICs is additionally subjected to severe financial hardship due to poverty, lack of gainful employment and the complete absence of old age income security benefits in many of these countries.

Amid the rising incidence of cancer illness, there is encouraging evidence that much can be done in every country to prevent, cure, and relieve the suffering (WHO 2002). Research has shown that at least 50 percent of cancers are preventable. Countries' experience show that no matter what resource constraints a country faces, a well-conceived, well-managed national cancer control programme is able to reduce cancer incidence and improve the lives of people living with cancer (WHO 2002). Science backed evidence suggests an important role of diet factors, such as a high intake of vegetables and fruits as a component of daily diet in containing the risks of cancer. These prevention efforts warrant attention beginning at prenatal and nascent years and continue through all life stages.

Key words: *cancer, non-communicable diseases, financial protection, productivity in the pharmaceutical industry, R&D efficiency, R&D effectiveness, value-based pricing, ICER, out-of-pocket expenses, social protection floor, ILO, OECD, WHO, differential pricing, sick leave benefits, DALY, patents, cash prize proposals, non-standard jobs, precarious employment, OECD countries, India, China*

Disclaimer

Due care has been taken to cite and credit the published research papers and sources used in this publication. The author apologizes for any inadvertent errors or omissions and requests that you bring to his attention any discrepancy in this regard.

The opinions expressed in this article solely represent those of the author's and do not reflect the views of the organizations cited. Correspondence concerning this paper should be addressed to Ramesh Bhardwaj, George Brown College, Toronto.

Contact: rbhardwa@georgebrown.ca

ACRONYMS and ABBREVIATIONS

ASIR: age-standardized incidence rates
BRICS: Brazil, Russian Federation, India, China and South Africa
CER: Cost Effectiveness Research
HIC: High Income Countries
HPV: Human papilloma virus
H pylori: Helicobacter pylori
IARC: International Agency for Research on cancer
ICER: Incremental Cost effective ratio
ILO: International Labor Organization
LIMCs: Low and Middle-Income Countries
NCD: Non-Communicable Diseases
NDA/BLA: New Drug Application/ and Biologics License Application
NICE: National Institute for Health and Care Excellence
NME: New Molecular entity
OECD: The Organization for Economic Co-operation and Development
OOP: out-of-pocket
QALY: Quality-adjusted life-year
WHO: World Health Organization
YLL: Years of Life Lost
TLD: Years Lived with Disability

Table of Contents

1. Introduction and Problem Statement

The advances in genetic re-engineering, gene sequencing, diagnostics and immunotherapy have resulted in a continuous decline in death rates and improvement in survival rates[1] around the globe in recent decades. As per the WHO report (2018), there has been an increasing trend in the survival rate during the 15-year period from 2000 due to two factors: (i) improvement in overall advancement in cancer care (i.e. early detection, improvement in pathology, surgery, radiotherapy, pharmacological treatments and other supportive care) and (ii) the availability of more effective treatments today for patients with better managed toxicity than in the previous decade in many countries. According to the American Cancer Society, as of 2015 the cancer death rate for men and women combined had fallen 26% from its peak in 1991.[2] However, despite the fact that there have been tremendous strides in the knowledge and understanding surrounding cancer illness, the new cases[3] continue to climb. Estimated new cases worldwide, in terms of age standardized incidence rates, have increased from 182.3 (per 100,000 population) in 2012 to 197.9 in 2018, both sexes, all ages (GLOBOCAN 2012. 2018).[4] New cases and new deaths are projected to be 15 million and 10 million respectively in 2020 even if current incidence rates and survival rates remain unchanged (Parkin 2000). Due to the rising incidence, cancer has now become the second leading cause of death worldwide (Fitzmaurice et al 2017). Redeeming, however, is the fact that many types of cancers are preventable, and as a consequence, the prevention of the risk factors as a strategic element of public health policy can have a significant impact.

It is estimated that over 2012–2016, the per-capita expenditure on cancer medicines had been about 2- to 8-fold above the overall per-capita expenditure on health, when using new cases of cancer as a proxy for treatment population (WHO 2018 Technical Report). Using a baseline scenario of constant cancer incidence, survival, and cost of care in the United States, Mariotto et al 2011 has estimated that the national costs of cancer care are expected to rise by 27% in 2020 from 2010. According to these authors, this represents a central challenge for both the federal government and the private sector. Costs are further likely to surge as new and more advanced treatments are adopted as standards of care. The soaring price of cancer drugs also raises some nagging concerns. First, in many cases, new drugs with high price tags offer minor improvements in terms of prolonging patients' lives. Second, people below the median income level will often not seek treatment, become financially bankrupt as the direct result of out-of-pocket (OOP) expenses (Correra et al 2018), or be left with a significant "toll" on their income and financial resources because of the combination of premiums and deductibles. Third, the absence of adequate financial protection in the form of paid sick leave and the subsequent income loss arising from physical debility seriously jeopardizes the recovery process. Finally, the working poor —those working under temporary employment contracts, in involuntary part-time jobs, or self-employed—may face catastrophic OOP expenses in the absence of work-related health insurance protection benefits.

LMICs face additional serious issues. In these countries, cancer drug prices are disproportionately high in relation to the country's per capita income level. Also, in most of these countries, a large majority of people are self-employed in the informal sector with no pensionable benefits from the government. Old age security is nonexistent in many of these countries. In the absence of a universal health care system and public funding, the major source of health financing is personal wealth, which, in most cases makes treatment completely unaffordable.

Low productivity and rising R&D costs are among the niggling challenges facing the pharmaceutical industry to its business model (Paul et al 2010, Woodcock & Woosley 2008). Despite rising investment in pharmaceutical research and development, successful development of novel drugs is slowing. Paul et al elaborates the issue of R&D productivity in two important dimensions: R&D efficiency (inputs leading to outputs) and R&D effectiveness (outputs leading to outcomes).

Figure 1 provides a pictorial view of suggested measures for restraining the costs of cancer drugs through improving productivity and regulatory reforms. An attempt is made to cover these issues and present the discussion as per the following sections.

Section two presents evidence on the incidence and disease burden measured in "disability-adjusted" life years (DALYs) at the regional level. This section also discusses the preventable risk factors.

Section three briefly describes how the escalating prices of cancer drugs can have financially devastating effects on economically poor people (including the working poor) in both developed and developing countries. The staggering costs of cancer drugs have raised concerns about access to treatments, protection against the risks of income loss, and financial insolvency from illness to recovery.

Section four and five explain the factors that potentially can restrain the rising trends of high prices. Section four examines the proposal of pricing based upon "Value-based" assessment of cancer drugs. In this case, research studies recommend the use of the incremental cost-effectiveness ratio (ICER) and the comparative effectiveness review (CER) approaches for aligning the therapeutic value with new drug prices. This section additionally stresses the need for stimulation competition through promoting cheaper generics, biologic and biosimilars products at the expiry of costly name-brand drugs. The proposal for delinking medicine prices from R&D cost, by introducing some program such as innovation inducement 'Prizes' as opposed to monopoly rights granted by patents, is briefly presented.

Section five deals with the economic challenge of decreasing R&D productivity trends in the pharmaceutical industry since 1970s. Declining cost efficiency (reflecting in a high attrition rates for oncology drugs after entering phase ii or phase iii trials, and high R&D costs per fewer 'New Molecular Entities'), as well as questionable value effectiveness of newly produced drugs are acting as major stumbling blocks to productivity increase and contributory factors to the escalating costs. Productivity crisis in the pharmaceutical R&D highlights the need for modernizing drug development process, as well for calls for radical reforms in the traditional regulatory approval process. These aspects are covered in this section.

Aside from the need to improve R&D efficiency, analysts have identified the need to improve the cost-effectiveness of new drug development and have also called for aligning the therapeutic value with new drug prices. The use of the incremental cost-effectiveness ratio (ICER) and the comparative effectiveness review (CER) approaches are advocated to improve the R&D effectiveness of new drugs. Often highly-priced new drugs do not represent commensurate benefits or significant therapeutic benefits relative to the predecessor drug. To amend this anomalous situation, proposals are put forward to delink drug prices from R&D costs.

Section six examines policies for limiting OOP expenses and for shielding patients against financial toxicity. Cancer patients experience the ordeal of financial toxicity during illness and the survival period as well. Financial toxicity is defined as the objective financial burden and subjective financial distress of patients with cancer. To compensate for loss of income due to sickness, the ILO (International Labor Organization) has advocated for the implementation of a universal social health protection strategy to deal with such inimical events. The principles of universal social health protection coverage aim to remove financial barriers to health services and protect people from the impoverishing effects of medical expenditures. This section reviews the financial protection policies in developed countries.

Section seven focuses on the special problems facing LMICs. This section highlights the need for nationally defined social protection floors that provide essential health care services and basic income security to all, including the informal sector poor and the elderly. This section also compares the relative performance of India and China in addressing human rights issues related to the health and income security of people.

Section eight presents discussion on prevention strategy to reduce the incidence and occurrence of cancer illness, both in developed and developing countries. The discussion in this section is mainly limited to primary prevention policies. The study is summarized and concluded in section nine.

Figure 1. Model of Efficient and Effective Drug Development Process

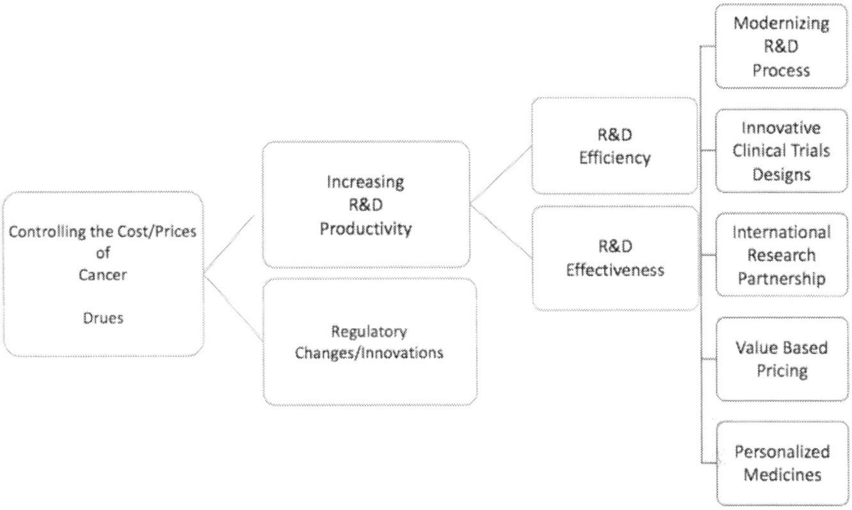

2. Incidence, Mortality and Morbidity: An Overview across Broad Economic Regions of the World

Cancer incidence rates have increased in most countries since 1990. Between 1990 and 2013, age-standardized incidence rates for all cancers combined (excluding non-melanoma skin cancer and Kaposi sarcoma) increased by more than 10% in 113 countries and decreased by more than 10% in 12 of 188 countries (Fitzmaurice, Dicker et al. 2013). Less developed and economically transitioning countries are at a higher risk of prevalence, particularly due to their slow pace in controlling cancer-causing infection at the population level coupled with their poorly resourced health systems in coping with the burden of expensive cancer treatments (Fitzmaurice et al 2017). Of the 14.9 million worldwide cancer cases, 8.2 million cancer deaths, and 196.3 million DALY's,5 developing countries partook 56% of incident cases, 62% of deaths, and 70% of DALYs in 2013 (Fitzmaurice et al, Global Burden of Disease Cancer Collaboration, 2015). The projected increase in cancer incidence by 2030 is estimated to be greater in low income (82%) and LMICs (70%) compared to the forecast for upper-middle (58%) and HICs (40%) (Evans et al., 2010). In case of screening and/or treatment of ailments such as female breast, colorectal, and certain childhood cancers, there are large survival differences between economically developed and developing countries (American Cancer Society, 2015).

LMICs are disproportionately affected by infectious agents that cause cancer, such as the human papilloma virus (HPV) which can lead to cervical cancer, Helicobacter pylori (H pylori) which can lead to stomach cancer, and

Hepatitis B and C, which can lead to liver cancer. Cancer-causing infections such as hepatitis and HPV are responsible for up to 25% of cancer cases in LMICs (WHO 2017, Cancer Facts Sheets). Moreover, cancer tends to be diagnosed at later stages in many developing countries compared to developed countries. This delayed diagnosis, combined with reduced access to appropriate therapeutic facilities and drugs, has adverse effects on survival rates in developing countries (Jemal et al., 2011).

2.1 Incidence and Burden of Cancer by Broad Regions

As per current evidence, new cancer cases (total and incidence rate)[6] are on the rise in all regions of the world. The global cancer study by Fitzmaurice and colleagues (2017) estimated that age-standardized incidence rates for all cancer cases increased by 33% between 2005 and 2015 in 174 of 195 countries or territories. The following table 1 from GLOBOCAN studies on cancer research reinforces the same trend, for all cancers combined (excluding non-melanoma skin cancers) for North America, Europe and the world.[7] In most studies, the incidence data are derived from population-based cancer registries (PBCR).

Globally, there is a large geographical diversity in cancer occurrence and the variations in between (and within, not shown here) world regions (see Table 1). The current data shows that Europe accounts for 23.4% of the global cancer cases although it has only 9.0% of the global population. The Americas, on the other hand, have 13.3% of the global population and account for 21.0% of incidence (International Agency for Research on Cancer, Press Release September 2018). In contrast to developed world regions, the proportions of incident cases each year in Asia and Africa stands at 48.4% and 5.8%, respectively (IARC, Press Release 2018, GLOBOCAN Database 2018). Cancer incidence is expected to increase in the future in LMICs as a result of the continuing epidemiological transition and life-style changes in developing nations (Fitzmaurice et al 2017).

Since many of the known causes of cancer are avoidable, it is possible to reduce the incidence rates of many types of cancer (Ames et al 1995). It is consoling to note that age-standardized death rates (ASDRs) for all cancers combined decreased within that same timeframe (1950-2015) in 140 of 195 countries or territories (Fitzmaurice et. al 2017). With the major exception of

African region, other countries experienced a decrease in cancer mortality despite increasing incidence rates between 2005 and 2015. The increase in the survival rates in developed regions, to a great extent, has been due to the spread of knowledge about the risk factors, timely access to specialized care, effective treatment, and good insurance coverage status among developed countries (Fitzmaurice and colleagues, 2017). Increasing cancer mortality rates in Sub-Saharan Africa is attributed to its weak health care infrastructure to treat cancer.

Table 1. Age standardized incidence of all sites cancer (excluding non-melanoma skin cancers) for selected Regions: 2012-2018

Age-standardized incidence rate of all cancers, per 100,000	2012 Both Sexes	2018 Both Sexes
Australia/New Zealand	318.5	463
North America	315.6	350.2
Western Europe	277.4	323.3
Northern Europe	298.7	316.3
Southern Europe	253.6	278.4
Central and Eastern Europe	216.1	238.3
World	182.3	197.9

Source: Globocan2018, Ferlay et al 2015; Torre et al 2015 (Global Cancer Statistics 2012)

2.2 Burden of Cancer

DALYs (per '000 population) due to cancer have remained unchanged over the 16-year period (2000-2016) at the global level (See Table 2). The stability in the DALYs at the global level is attributed to falling rates for Hodgkin lymphoma, cervical, stomach, larynx, nasopharynx, gallbladder, biliary tract, esophageal, and bladder cancers (Global Burden of Disease Cancer Collaboration, 2015). Moreover, in recent years, 84% of the countries in the world are reported to have had funding for early detection and screening for NCDs, and 89% of countries had funding for providing health care for NCDs, as well as for primary prevention and health promotion (Evans et al., 2010). Another contributory factor to stable DALYs is the increased attention being directed to preventive measures, such as addressing problems of obesity, smoking, alcohol consumption, and hypertension, and there is growing use of early screening and detection measures in most countries. Increased attention toward immunization programs against infection-related cancers is an additional safeguard to contain DALYs related to cancer.

Globally, it is reported that by 2012, the probability of dying from one of the four main NCDs between ages 30–70 had been reduced by an estimated 19%, while the death rate for the four main NCDs in the same population was reduced by 23% (World Health Organization, 2014). In developed countries, continuing medical advances are helping to reduce the incidence rate and to improve the survival rate from cancer in near future. The evidence shows that overall U.S. cancer incidence from 1999-2013 has continued to decrease for men and remain stable for women (National Cancer Institute, 2017; Siegel et al., 2016).

However, with population aging and the epidemiological transition, the global cancer incidence rate is poised to increase in the future (Fitzmaurice and Akinyemiju, et al. 2018). Since the countries belonging to different economic groups are at different stages of demographic and epidemiologic transitions, it may be useful to consider the distribution of disability burden by age. It has been estimated that aging contributed 20% to 43% of the absolute increase in incident cases between 1990 and 2013 (Global Burden of Disease Cancer Collaboration, 2015). The incidence of cancer among older adults is reported to be nearly ten times the rate for those less than 65-years old (Davidoff et al., 2013). Evidence shows that the number of older persons—those aged 60 years or over—has increased substantially in recent years in most countries. In 2015, one in eight people worldwide was aged 60 years or over (UN 2015 b).

Table 2. DALYs (per '000 population) **Attributable to Cancer Illness:** *By Economic Regions- Estimates for 2000-2016*

Economic Regions	2000	2016
Low Income	21	21
Low Middle Income	21	22
Upper Middle Income	39	39.6
High Income	52	50.1
Global	33	32.7

Source: WHO: Health statistics and information Systems, Disease Burden

Another reason for considering the importance of age in the disability burden of cancer is the age-related incidence of many cancers. Evidence shows that certain cancers like Mesothelioma, non-Hodgkin lymphoma, thyroid, prostate, breast, colon, rectal, and pancreatic cancers, have a higher incidence rate in older patients (Global Burden of Disease Cancer Collaboration, 2015). Other cancers are more common in younger age groups, such as Hodgkin lymphoma, leukemia, and testicular, brain, and nervous system cancers, where population aging does not contribute to an increase in incident cases (Global Burden of Disease Cancer Collaboration 2015).

In consideration of the above factors, Table 3 presents data for the burden of cancer across different economic regions (four World Bank income groups) and for different age categories for 2000 and 2015. There are variations in the burden of cancer across the regions by age distribution. The data show a higher burden of cancer in upper-middle income countries and HICs for people in the above 70 age group compared to the burden observed in low-income countries. The declining birth rate (in developed European countries and Japan) and significant medical advancements have improved longevity and thereby accelerated the aging process in most of the developed economic regions. Globally, while most of the cancer burden still comes from years of life lost (YLLs) rather than years lived with disability (YLDs), reflecting a higher burden of deaths than disability (Fitzmaurice, Akinyemiju, et al 2018), cancer survivorship, on the other hand, is also increasing due to the rapid advancements in cancer therapies. The improvement in the survivorship in developed countries is reflected in the higher prevalence rates found in those countries.[8] Evidence confirms that along with the aging trend, the 5-year prevalence rate of cancer has increased in developed economic regions. Due to the increasing prevalence, the YLD[9] component of DALYs is resulting in a high cancer burden in older age groups. With life expectancy increasing globally, the future burden of cancer is likely to increase, unless incidence rates fall substantially.

Table 3. Comparison of Burdens of Cancer (DALY per 1000 population) by age group, 2015

Region	Age (years)						
	<5	5–14	15–29	30–49	50–59	60–69	>70
Low income	5.8	3.5	9.1	36.6	82.0	113.0	125.2
Low-middle income	4.6	3.2	5.9	25.3	68.1	96.3	97.8
Upper-middle income	6.3	3.8	5.8	24.1	76.6	129.1	186.7
High income	2.8	2.2	3.4	17.7	71.6	129.0	176.5
Global	5.1	3.3	5.9	24.3	73.0	119.1	159.8

Source: WHO: Health statistics and information Systems, Disease Burden

Since much of the burden of cancer incidence, morbidity, and mortality is estimated to occur in the developing world (Kanavos 2006), it is essential to prioritize controlling the cancer risk factors in these countries. Public health policies that scale up prevention measures in LMICs with limited resources are likely to be more effective in containing the formidable challenge of cancer illness than spending resources on treatment alone. In a war against cancer, the study by 'Global Burden of Disease Cancer Collaboration (2017)' has highlighted the need for prevention efforts such as tobacco control measures, accelerated vaccination efforts, promotion of physical activity and healthy dietary lifestyles.

2.3 Cancer Risk Factors

Decades of basic, epidemiological, and clinical research have led to the identification of numerous risk factors (American Cancer Society Report 2018) that play a role in the development of different types of cancers. Research findings suggest that nearly all cancers originate from both environmental and genetic factors, meaning that there are multiple external factors combined with internal genetic changes that can lead to human cancers (Parsa 2012). Research studies also indicate that approximately one-half of all cancer cases either arise from modifiable risk factors or can be detected as precursor lesions before the development of disease with metastatic potential (WHO 2018 Cancer Factsheet #297). Doll and Peto (1981) in their review of avoidable risks of cancer in the United States, attributed 30% of cancer deaths to tobacco and roughly 35% to dietary factors although the plausible contribution of diet ranged from 10% to 70%. The modifiable risk factors have been dichotomized as either lifestyle or environmental (White et al 2014). These are briefly reviewed below.

Lifestyle and behavior related modifiable risk factors include (WHO 2007, WHO 2002)[10]:

- tobacco use
- alcohol use
- dietary factors including low fruit and vegetable intake
- physical inactivity
- overweight and obesity

Environmental related risk factors include exposure to:

- physical carcinogens, such as ultraviolet (UV) and ionizing radiation;
- chemical carcinogens, such as benzo(a)pyrene, formaldehyde and aflatoxins (food contaminants), and fibres such as asbestos;
- biological carcinogens, such as infections by viruses, bacteria and parasites.

Lifestyle Related Risk Factors

It is estimated that around one third of deaths from cancer are due to the 5 leading behavioral and dietary risks. These are high body mass index, low fruit and vegetable intake, lack of physical activity, tobacco use, and alcohol use (WHO 2018 Cancer Factsheet #297).

Tobacco Use as a Risk Factor

Doll and Peto (1981) listed cigarette smoking as the major single preventable cause of cancer in the United States, and as per their estimates cigarette smoking accounted for about 30% of all cancer deaths in 1978. These authors observed that the ratio of the death rate among cigarette smokers to that among lifelong non-smokers of comparable age was, for men under 70 years, about 2:1, while for men over 70 years it was about 1.5:1. Medical research studies have noted that smoking causes oxidation[11] of macromolecules[12] and deplete antioxidant levels (Ames et al 1993), thus become a precursor to a variety of risk factors. Scientific evidence warns that tobacco smoke damages not just DNA but also the proteins in cells that repair DNA damage. Smoking also interferes with a process called metabolic detoxification, in which cells neutralize some toxins and flush the harmless byproducts out of the body. Empirical data suggest that tobacco use, in addition to causing about 90% of lung cancer, contributes to other cancers, such as mouth, esophagus, stomach, kidney, pancreas, bladder, leukemia, and possibly colon (Ames et al 1995).

Excessive Alcohol Consumption as a Risk Factor

Regarding the adverse effect of alcohol consumption, the World Cancer Research Fund/American Institute for Cancer Research (AICR) report stated there was convincing evidence that drinking alcohol was a cause of cancers of the oral cavity, pharynx, larynx, esophagus, breast, and colorectal (in men).[13] Heavy intake of alcoholic beverages is found to be associated with nutrient deficiency, which appears to contribute independently to oral carcinogenesis (Petersen 2009). Also, alcohol was found to be a probable cause of increased risk of liver cancer and colorectal cancer in women.

Combination of Alcohol and Cigarette Consumption: More Injurious

Studies have also reported that cancer risks in those who are both alcohol drinkers and cigarette smokers are much larger than the risks seen for those who only drink alcohol or only smoke cigarettes. Combined use of excessive alcohol and tobacco significantly increases the risk of cancers in the aero-digestive tract—the lips, mouth, larynx, pharynx, throat, esophagus and colon. According to a Senior Scientist, Frank New Port of Gallop Survey (2014),[14] "80 percent of throat and mouth cancer in men and 65 percent of throat and mouth cancer in women in the US" have been found to have links to the combination of smoking and drinking." Both excessive alcohol consumption and tobacco use provide evidence of an elevated risk of cancers of the oral cavity, esophagus, larynx, and respiratory tract (Plummer 1985, Doll and Peto).

Poor Dietary Habits, Overweight and Obesity as Risk Factors

Empirical evidence from United States has most strongly emphasized the inadequate attention to protective factors, rather than excessive intake of harmful factors, as major contributing factors (Ames et al 1995). For example, the low intake of vegetables and fruits acts as a great risk factor in several NCDs, particularly, cardiovascular disease and cancer (Lock et al 2005). Block, Patterson and Subar (1992) in their review of 200 studies, concluded that for most cancer sites (lung, colon, breast, cervix, esophagus, oral cavity, bladder, pancreas and ovary), persons with low fruit and vegetable intake experience about twice the risk of cancer compared with those with high intake, even after control for potentially confounding factors.

Lock et al (2005) suggest that increasing individual fruit and vegetable consumption to up to 600 g per day (the baseline of choice) has potential of reducing the burden of several cancers such as stomach, esophageal, lung and colorectal cancer by 19%, 20%, 12% and 2%, respectively. Key et al (2004) suggest that diets should include at least 400 g/d of total fruits and vegetables in order to reduce the risk of the oral cavity, esophagus, stomach and colorectum. The Dietary Guidelines for Americans 2010 recommend one-half of a plate fruits and vegetables (Salvin and Lloyd 2012). Salvin and Lloyd suggest that fiber is an active component of fruits and vegetables and a reason to continue to support their consumption. Steinmetz and Porter, in their study, examined prospective cohort studies,[15] case control studies[16] and study designs.[17] In their review, the types of vegetables or fruit that most often appear to be protective against cancer are raw vegetables, followed by allium vegetables, carrots, green vegetables, cruciferous vegetables, and tomatoes. Block et al 1991, in their review of 200 studies examined the relationship between fruit and vegetable intake and cancers of various sites. They found a statistically significant protective effect of fruit and vegetable consumption in 128 of 156 dietary studies in which results were expressed in terms of relative risk. Similar conclusions about the protective effect of vegetable and fruit consumption have been reported by Steinmetz and Potter (1996). In their review of 205 human epidemiology studies and 22 animal studies, Steinmetz and Potter found evidence for a protective effect of greater vegetable and fruit consumption consistent for cancers of the stomach, esophagus, lung, oral cavity and pharynx, endometrium, pancreas, and colon. Research spanning three decades suggests that grass-based diets can significantly improve the fatty acid (FA) composition and antioxidant content of beef (Daley et al 2010). Of note, it has been observed that Seventh-Day Adventists, who generally do not smoke, drink heavily, or eat much meat but do eat a diet rich in fruits and vegetables, have overall cancer mortality about half that of the general U.S. population (Ames et al 1995).

Dietary antioxidants slow down the aging process (Ames et al 1993, Poljsak et al 2013a). Since aging is the result of excessive production of ROS (reactive oxygen species)[18] and reduced antioxidant defense, increased intake of fruits and vegetables along with regular physical activity and reduced calorie intake can help to reduce oxidative damage (important contributor to human aging) (Poljsak and Milisav 2013b). For providing some protection against age degeneration causes, *in vitro* and *in vivo* studies[19] suggest that antioxidant nutrients and related bioactive compounds from fruits and vegetables can protect people from oxidative stress (Poljsak et al 2013a). Research studies have also highlighted the potential dietary factors in reversing gene expression or other modifications due to the aging factor. Antioxidants are now being examined as persuasive therapeutics against age-related degenerative diseases like cancer.

Studies have also indicated that in addition to fruits and vegetables, the low ratio of polyunsaturated fatty acids (PUFA) to saturated fatty acid is considered as one of the risk factors.

Meat is seen to be a major source of saturated fatty acids (Wood et al 2003). Red meat, such as beef, lamb and pork has been classified as a 'probable' cause of cancer (WHO 2015).[20] Robust evidence of association between incidence of colorectal cancer (which is the third most commonly diagnosed cancer, after lung and female breast cancer) (WHO 2018), red meat, and poor intake of a fibrous vegetarian diet suggest that cancer incidence may be reduced by changing the proportion of plant based food and animal fat in diet. The World Health Organization (WHO) has cautioned that processed meat was a major contributor to colorectal cancer, classifying it as "carcinogenic to humans" (WHO's Press Release, 26 October 2015). It is reported that just one hot dog or a few strips of bacon consumed daily increases cancer risk by 18 percent

(Physicians Committee for Responsible Medicine 2018, Processed Meat), showing that there is no safe amount of processed meat. In a population-based study, Irwin et al (2005) found that obese women and women who gain weight after a breast cancer diagnosis are at a greater risk for breast cancer recurrence and death compared with lean women and women who do not gain weight. It is suggested that body weight should be maintained in the body mass index range of 18.5-25 kg/m^2, and weight gain in adulthood avoided (Key et al 2004). Physical activity, the main determinant of energy expenditure, reduces the risk for colorectal cancer and probably reduces the risk for breast cancer (Key et al 2004).

Studies have also alluded to the production and consumption of the red meat being one of the major contributors to methane gas in the environment, leading to the greenhouse effect. Evidence shows that in contrast to general trends of GHG (Greenhouse Gas) emissions, carbon dioxide (CO_2) is only a small component of emissions in animal agriculture. The largest share of GHG emissions is from two other gases: methane (CH_4) and nitrous oxide (N_2O). Globally, about 9 percent of emissions in the entire agricultural sector consist of CO_2, 35-45 percent consists of methane and 45-55 percent consists of nitrous oxide (UNEP 2012). Cattle are considered by far the largest contributors to global enteric CH_4 emissions, as they are the most numerous and have a much larger body size relative to other species such as sheep and goats (UNEP 2012).

Table 4. Average Greenhouse Gas Emissions Per Unit Protein Carbon-dioxide Equivalent Per Gram of Protein

Entity	CO2 per gram of protein 2017
Beef/Mutton	221.63
Fresh Produce	37.17
Pork	36.33
Rice	21.16
Wheat	4.6
Pulses	0.58

Source: Our World in Data, Meat, Seafood, Production and consumption Diet and medicinal herbs (e.g., turmeric and others) are a major source of antioxidants.

Exposure to Environmental Risk Factors

Environmental contaminants are considered to be another group of risk factors. Environmental risk factors can be grouped under two categories: (i) exposure to physical and chemical carcinogens, and (ii) exposure to cancer causing infections (pathogens).

Exposure to Physical and Chemical Carcinogens

Environmental pollutants are non-infectious sources of chronic inflammation that contribute to various pathological conditions that can lead to cancer (Ames et al 1993). Air pollution, mostly caused by transport, power generation, industrial or agricultural emissions, as well as residential heating and cooking, is already known to raise risks for a wide range of illnesses. The IARC has classified outdoor air pollution as a cancer-causing agent (carcinogen). In its evaluation, the IARC concluded that outdoor air pollution causes lung cancer and is also linked to an increased risk for bladder cancer. Evidence shows that exposure to occupational agents including asbestos (used by industry, construction, and commercial sectors) can cause chronic inflammation and be a risk factor for lung cancer (Ames 1993). The findings by Luo et al (2011) suggest that environmental exposure to chromium, formaldehyde, and nickel from TRI (Toxic release inventory) sites may increase population risk of lung cancer. Another pollutant, an invisible gas called radon, can seep into homes from the ground where it has been found to increase the risk of lung cancer.

Exposure to ultraviolet (UV) radiation has been found to be a risk factor that causes skin cells to become cancer cells. Evidence shows that the depletion of stratospheric ozone leads to an increase in UV exposure and temperature, increasing the risk of skin cancer and cataracts. $CO_2$from the combustion of fossil fuels and biomass for energy use is designated as a major contributor to the enhanced greenhouse effect. Health hazards of exposures to respirate fibers of asbestos at work places have also been reported by the U.S. Environmental Protection Agency (EPA) and other research studies.

Children are found to be more vulnerable than adults to many chemicals, partly because of the biologic sensitivity that is an inherent characteristic of early growth and development (Landrigan et al 2002). More rigorous research is needed on a range of emerging environmental health issues (Briggs 2003) and their effects on the human metabolic system.

Infectious Agents and Cancer

Infections by bacteria, parasites, or viruses and tissue inflammation such as gastritis, hepatitis, and colitis are recognized risk factors for human cancers at various sites (Ohshima & Bartsch (1994, Plummer et al 2016). Some viruses can disrupt signaling that normally keeps cell growth and proliferation in check. Also, some infections weaken the immune system, making the body less able to fight off other cancer-causing infections. And some viruses, bacteria, and parasites also cause chronic inflammation, which may lead to cancer. There are ten infectious agents that have been classified as carcinogenic to humans (Group 1) by the International Agency for Research on Cancer (IARC). These include, one bacterium (Helicobacter pylori), six viruses (e.g., hepatitis B virus (HBV), hepatitis C virus (HCV), and others), and three parasites. Human immunodeficiency virus (HIV) was not considered separately because it only causes cancer through immune-suppression by enhancing the carcinogenic action of other viruses. To reduce the infection related cancers, population-based vaccination and screen-and-treat programs are suggested to be accessible (Plummer et al 2012). Of the 12.7 million new cancer cases that occurred in 2008, the population attributable fraction (PAF) for infectious agents was 16.1%, meaning that around 2 million new cancer cases that year were attributable to infections (de Martel et al 2012). This fraction was higher in less developed countries (22.9%) than in more developed countries (7.4%). Hepatitis and human papilloma virus (HPV), have been found to be responsible for up to 25% of cancer cases in LMICs (WHO 2018, Cancer Fact sheet #297). The following table 5 provides information about the geographic distribution of cancers linked to infectious agents.

Table 5. Proportion of Cancers Attributable to Infection by World Regions 2012

Regions	Attributable to infections (Percentage)
North America	4
Oceania	5
Europe	7
North Africa and West Africa	13
Latin America	14
Central Asia	19
East Asia	23
Sub-Saharan Africa	31
World	15

Source: American Cancer Society (Global Cancer, Facts and Figures 4th edition

Advancing ge as Risk Factor

While cancer can strike anyone—at any age, gender, race, ethnicity, socio-economic status -- it has been found that certain segments of the population shoulder a disproportionate burden of cancer. Epidemiological evidence shows advancing age is the most important risk factor for cancer overall, and for many individual cancer types as mentioned previously (National Cancer Institute, NIH USA 2015). In the European Union (EU), estimates show that one third of all new cases were diagnosed in people aged 75 years or older in 2012, and one half of all cancer deaths occurred in this age group. In the United States, 87% of all cancers are diagnosed in people 50 years of age or older (American Cancer Society, 2017: Cancer Facts and figures). In a global study of incidence and burden of 32 cancers in 195 countries from 1990 to 2015, Fitzmaurice and colleagues (2017) found that age as a factor exerted a prime influence on several types of cancer. With improvements in the life expectancy, many countries are experiencing an increase in older individuals, both in terms of absolute numbers and as a proportion of the total population. White et al

(2014) have suggested the role of epigenetic alterations such as DNA methylation in the complex aging process as an emerging area of research. Medical advances hold a promise of slowing down the rate of aging and reducing the associated disease burden.

2.4 Model: An Empirical Analysis of Selected Risk Factors in OECD Countries

As reported by several research studies, the increasing incidence of cancer at the global level is attributable to several factors, including population growth and aging (Fitzmaurice and colleagues, 2017) as well as to environmental and lifestyle changes associated with social and economic development. Epidemiological evidence from developed nations has suggested higher probability of cancer incidence in the old age population, tobacco users, heavy alcohol consumers, and people with obesity along with poor dietary habits. The present study uses data of developed OECD countries, which allow us to control the influence of multiple economic and social factors, such as the stage of epidemiological transition, the level of economic development and lifestyle factors. Based upon the above information about the risk factors, the present study has attempted to analyze the effect of age (percentage of population above 70), and lifestyle risk factors as predictors of cancer incidence in OECD countries.

In our empirical analysis, the prevalence of the cancer rate in the population was regressed on each country's proportion of population above the age of 70 years and consumption of red meat (kg per capita), using data of OECD countries. In most studies, researchers utilize data on the age-standardized rates (ASRs) in order to facilitate comparisons of cancer incidence and prevalence through an indicator that is independent of the age profile of each population. This study, however, has used non-standardized data since the age variable is used as an explanatory variable. The other problem of using standardized rates is the need to select an arbitrary standard population for age standardization, which is representative of neither the present nor the future age-specific global population (Bray et al 2002). The results of linear regression are presented below.

Results:

Before interpreting the result, it is important to keep in mind that the incidence of cancer depends upon several complex and interdependent factors. With our limited cross-sectional data of OECD countries, we could find only two statistically significant predictors. In interpreting the goodness of fit, the limited availability of comparable data is one important limitation in our study.

In statistical analysis, one measure of the goodness of fit is R or R^2. $R^2 = \frac{SSm}{SSt} = 0.366$; where SSm represents the amount of variance in the cancer incidence explained by our model (independent variables), and SS*t* refers to total sum of square (the difference between the observed value and the values predicted by the mean of the variable. The second measure is to use sum of squares in assessing the F-test. We find from the table that F ratio to be significant at $p \leq 0.001$.

Table 6. Output: Ordinary Least Square (OLS)

Output Table A

Model Summary									
					Change Statistics				
Model	R	R Square	Adjusted R Square	Std. Error of the Estimate	R Square Change	F Change	df1	df2	Sig. F Change
1	.605a	.366	.324	.813188	.366	8.657	2	30	.001
a. Predictors: (Constant), Meat kg/per, Pop above 70									

Output Table B

ANOVA[a]						
Model		Sum of Squares	df	Mean Square	F	Sig.
1	Regression	11.449	2	5.725	8.657	.001b
	Residual	19.838	30	.661		
	Total	31.287	32			
a. Dependent Variable: Incidence cancer Globocan						
b. Predictors: (Constant), Meat kg/per, Pop above 70						

While the above ANOVA (in Table 6 B) result tell us whether the overall model results in significantly good degree of prediction of the outcome (dependent) variable, we also require details of individual contribution of variables in the model (Field 2016). From the Output Table 6C, it is found that population above the age of 70 is quite a significant predictor, and the consumption of red meat is moderately significant explanatory variable. Both the variables have right expected signs. Our results are quite consistent with the available clinical and epidemiological evidence. The significance of advancing age as a risk factor in cancer incidence has been demonstrated in biological and empirical research studies (Balducci and Extermann 2000; Berger et al 2006; Aunan et al 2017). The IARC of the WHO has classified processed meat as a "definite" cause of cancer, or a Group 1 carcinogen – the same group that includes smoking and alcohol. The latest research shows that eating more than 18 ounces of red meat per week increases the risk of colorectal cancers (CRC) (American Institute for Cancer Research, Red and Processed Meat).[21] Worldwide, CRC is the third most common cancer in men and the second in women. More than half of these global cases occur in more developed countries (Aykan 2005).

Output Table C Collinearity Statistics

Model		Unstandardized Coefficients		Standardized Coefficients Beta	t	Sig	Collinearity Statistics Tolerance	VIF
		B	Std. Error					
1	(Constant)	2.014	1.023		1.968	.058		
	Pop above 70	26.208	7.340	.523	3.571	.001	.984	1.016
	Meat cons kg/per	.014	.005	.377	2.572	.015	.984	1.016

Output: Partial Least Squares Regression (PLSR)

Output Table D

Parameters	
Independent Variables	Dependent Variables Incidence cancer
(Constant)	2.012
Pop above70	26.943
Red Meat cons kg/per	.013

Since our data set has limited observations, covering only 25 countries, we decided to examine the OLS estimates through using Partial Least Square regression (PLSR) approach, which is particularly considered useful when we need to predict a set of dependent variables from a (very) large set of independent variables (i.e., predictors) (Abdi 2007). PLSR is a technique that generalizes and combines features from principal component analysis and multiple regression (Abdi 2007).

Relative Importance Analysis: Variable Importance in the Projection (VIP) of Cancer Incidence

VIP coefficients represent the importance of each X variable in fitting both the X- and Y-scores, since the Y-scores are predicted from the X-scores.[22] The higher a variable's VIP score, the more influential it is in determining the PLSR model for both predictors and responses. Although VIP cut-off points vary throughout the literature, traditionally variables with VIP scores lower than 0.8 are deemed as non-influential in the model. As per the threshold set by Wold (1994) at 0.8, the present exercise has found the role of the age as the probable predictor of cancer incidence in OECD countries. The red meat consumption as a predictor falls short (by a small margin) of the recommended rule of thumb. Parameter estimates are the regression coefficients, and the sign of the coefficients indicates the direction of the effect. In our estimates, all coefficients have expected signs.

Typically, X-weights and X-loadings are similar in sign. From loadings, it is obvious that factor 1 in our weights and loading tables, is heavily associated with the age factor. By one rule of thumb in confirmatory PLS factor analysis, loadings should be 0.7 or higher to confirm that independent variables identified a priori are represented by a particular factor (SmartPLS 2016). However, some researchers, particularly for exploratory purposes, use a lower level such as .4 for the central factor and .25 for other factors (Raubenheimer, 2004, cited by Statnotes from North Carolina State University).

Output Table E

Variable Importance in the Projection	
Variables	Latent Factors
	1
Pop above70	1.184
Read Meat cons kg/per	.773
Cumulative Variable Importance	

Output Table F

Weights	
Variables	Latent Factors
	1
Pop above70	.837
Red Meat cons kg/per	.547
Incidence cancer	.643

Output Table G

Loadings	
Variables	Latent Factors
	1
Pop above70	.869
Red Meat cons kg/per	.499
Incidence cancer	1.000

Appendix: Partial Least Squares

Partial least squares (PLS; aka, Projection to Latent Structures) is a popular approach for analyzing high-dimensional data, viz., relating to problems in bioinformatics and genomics. Partial least squares is a method for constructing predictive models when the factors are many and highly collinear (Tobias, 2016). Partial least squares regression generalizes and combines features from principal component analysis and multiple regression. Its goal is to predict or analyze a set of dependent variables from a set of independent variables or predictors by extracting from the predictors a set of orthogonal factors called latent variables that have the best predictive power (Abdi, 2007). In nutshell, the X variables (the predictors) in PLS are reduced to principal components, as are the Y variables (the dependents). The components of X are used to predict the scores on the Y components, and the predicted Y component scores are used to predict the actual values of the Y variables.[23]

Both principal component regression (PCR) and PLSR techniques circumvent this by decomposing X into orthogonal scores and loadings. The major difference between PCR and PLSR is, while PCR uses only the variation of *X* to construct new factors, PLSR uses both the variation of *X* and *Y* to construct new factors that play the role of explanatory variables (Yeniay & Goktas, 2002).[24] The principle behind PLSR is to search for a set of latent vectors by performing a simultaneous decomposition of X and Y with the constraint that these components explain as much as possible of the covariance between X and Y (Zhao et al., 2013). That is, PLSR regression estimates regression parameters so that the variance of Y explained the explanatory variables are maximal. Assume *X* is a n×p matrix of predictor (independent) variables and *Y* is a n×q matrix (of dependent or response variables). The PLSR technique works by successively extracting factors from both X and Y such that covariance between the extracted factors is maximized. Both X and Y and are decomposed into scores and loadings in such a way that the covariance between and scores is maximized. Partial least squares do not need the data to come from normal or known distributions (Falk &Miller, 1992).

To regress the Y variables with the explanatory variables X1, . . ., Xp, PLSR attempts to find latent variables or components that play the same role as the Xs (Yeniay & Goktas, 2002). Assume *X* is a n×p matrix of predictor (independent) variables and *Y* is a n×q matrix (of dependent or response variables). The PLSR technique works by successively extracting factors from both X and Y such that covariance between the extracted factors is maximized. Partial least squares regression is based on the basic latent component decomposition (Boulesteix & Strimmer, 2007) as shown in Equations (1) and (2). That is, the PLSR technique tries to find a linear decomposition of X and Y such that

$$X = TP^T + E \qquad (1)$$

$$Y = UQ^T + F \qquad (2)$$

The matrix X is decomposed into a matrix T (the score matrix) and a matrix P (the loadings matrix) plus an error matrix E. The matrix Y is decomposed into U (score matrix), Q (the loadings matrix), and the error term F. These two equations are called outer relations (Geladi & Kowalski, 1986). The extracted factors (T) are used to predict the Y-scores (U), and then the predicted Y-scores are used to construct predictions for the responses (Tobias, 2016).

Decomposition is finalized to maximize covariance between T and U. There are multiple algorithms available to solve the PLSR problem. However, all algorithms follow an iterative process to extract the X-scores and Y-scores. (See details in Abdi, 2010; Maitra & Yan, 2008).

3. Escalating Costs, Financial Toxicity and Treatment Gap

Delivering quality and equitable care at affordable cost has become one of the burning and vexing issues in all countries, including HICs (Sullivan et al 2013). As a consequence of the sky-rocketing prices of new cancer drugs and substantial out-of-pocket cost barriers to accessing affordable care, the worldwide cost of cancer due to premature death and disability (excluding medical cost) could be staggering (Sullivan et al 2013) and unbearable for people in poorly resources countries. Many cancer patients are especially vulnerable financially because their illness impedes their ability to work, and sometimes even causes them to lose their employment altogether. Even with insurance coverage, cancer patients often experience financial hardships (arising from high premiums, deductibles, coinsurance, and copayments for covered services), debt, depletion of all assets to pay for cancer treatment, and personal bankruptcy (National Cancer policy Forum 2014).

There are growing concerns about developing nations' resources and their capacity to deal with the growing burden of cancer. Individual patients and caregivers with poor employment, financial, and insurance status in these poorly resourced countries experience numerous geographic and healthcare system challenges that result in eschewing treatment or reliance on traditional healers (Price et al 2012). More than 60 percent of the world's employed population is in the informal economy (ILO press release 2018). The majority of the people employed in the informal economy lack social protection, rights at work, and decent working conditions. This calls for, among other measures, a greater attention to make cancer treatment affordable and to provide timely access to patients across the globe. The high cost of cancer drugs is related to numerous factors ranging from the high cost of drug development (low R&D productivity), the use of monopoly power in the pricing of drugs, and to the prevalence of patent systems. The following discussion deals with each of these factors.

Continuing medical advances in the cancer drug arena have been accompanied by increases in the cost of treatment. While it is comforting to know that molecular and immune therapies have revolutionized cancer treatment and improved patient outcomes and survival, the high cost of new therapies has increased the burden of OOP expenses for patients, leading to poorer financial well-being, quality of life, psychosocial health, and treatment adherence (Tran and Zafar 2018). In their 2018 report to the President of the United States, the President's Cancer Panel raised the concern that "…virtually all new cancer drugs enter the market with a price tag that exceeds $100,000 per year and, increasingly, much higher." In the panel's view, drug costs are accelerating far faster than costs for other components of care, which, together, can result in financial toxicity[25], imposing a "significant burden on patients, including a diminished quality of life, interference with high quality care delivery, and even a reduction in survival rates." A study by Howard, Bach, Berndt, & Conti (2015), documented the escalation in cancer drug prices by an average of $8,500 per year over the past 15 years. According to their analysis, the cost of drugs for each additional year lived (after adjusting for inflation) has increased, from $54,000 in 1995 to $207,000 in 2013. Patients' advocates and caregivers have expressed concerns and frustrations about the poor relationship between new and often very costly cancer drugs and benefits obtained in terms of additional years of survival. Bach (2009) noted that in many cases, the magnitude of the increase in the cost of treatment exceeded the magnitude of improvement in efficacy limits on Medicare's ability to control rising spending on cancer drugs. When weighing prices against benefits, Howard et al. (2015) found that prices rose by 120% for each additional life year gained, or 14% per month of added life.

Imperfect Market Structure of Cancer Medicines

WHO (2018) reported evidence on 'The Herfindahl-Hirschman Index (HHI)' – a measure of market concentration – by which it can be found that three companies accounted for about 50% of the global market of cancer medicines by 2017 sales value, indicating that market structure of cancer medicines is characterized by imperfect competition.[26] This report has drawn attention to the price setting goals of pharmaceutical firms. Evidence compiled by the above report shows that pharmaceutical companies often place more emphasis on setting prices according to their income expectations, instead of setting prices according to the value of medicines. Pharmaceutical markets in particular function less well to align value, price, and cost, because necessary conditions are weaker. Patients, payers, and even physicians often lack good information about effectiveness and risks, especially for new drugs (Danzon and Taylor 2009)

Many price increases of cancer medicines over the past decades have been found to be unconnected to either the relative or absolute therapeutic value of the medicines, or the costs of R&D and production (WHO 2018 P21 for examples of medicine prices). One plausible explanation appears to be that the companies' attempt to reach their profit goals by setting prices as high as the market will bear (WHO 2018, Kantarjian & Rajkumar 2015, Kantarijan et al 2014). Monopoly power and pricing is partly explained by protection of intellectual property (patents) keeps generic or biosimilar competition out of the market for varying periods of time (See more details in WHO 2018). Patents and other market exclusivities limit competition in order to preserve incentives for research and development (R&D), but thereby also reduce competitive pressures on prices (Dazon and Taylor 2009).

The above mentioned pricing practice, based on "power imbalance" exists between patients and drug companies, often makes cancer medicines unaffordable, preventing the full benefit of the medicines from being realized (WHO 2018). Due to escalating costs, an estimated 10%–20% of U.S. patients with cancer compromise or forego their prescribed treatments (Tefferi et al., 2015). Even insured patients face an inordinate financial burden due to the market power of insurance companies, rising prices in the forms of higher insurance premiums and deductibles, additional coverage exclusions or limits, and increased copayments. WHO report (2018) has acknowledged that even in countries where "cost-containment measures" are in place, cancer drug treatments are "reduced, delayed, and even cancelled." High prices raise questions of crowd-out of other services in payer budgets, affordability of copayments to patients, and concern whether the health benefits gained warrant the high cost

(Danzon and Taylor 2009).

The surging costs of cancer drugs have raised widespread outrage among various stakeholders. In a *Mayo Clinic Proceedings* article, a group of 118 leading cancer experts expressed concern, suggested that patients be treated with innovative medicines, and made an impassioned plea for action, including a call for new regulations to control the high cost of cancer drugs (Tefferi, 2015). Cancer patients face a number of serious problems, including emotional and physiological stress, availability (or lack thereof) of effective treatment, and impending fear of financial impoverishment or physical disability resulting in lost work income.

3.1 Adverse Consequences of High Cost of Treatment

The shift toward high-priced improved drugs—which include most targeted therapies and immunotherapies—has substantially increased OOP costs for many patients (President's Cancer Panel 2018). Cancer-related drugs accounted for 26.6% of the cancer-related health-care cost on average in the European Union in 2009 (See table 1 in Luengo-Fernandez) and about 20 percent of the total costs of cancer care in the United States as per recent estimates (President's Cancer Panel 2018). The prices of many novel drugs make affordable access to them very difficult for both payers and patients.

Underinsured people in precarious jobs, younger patients, and those with lower household incomes are at higher risk of treatment-related financial hardship (President's Cancer Panel 2018). Soaring prices and significant OOP spending on drugs raise questions of crowd-out of other services in payer budgets, affordability of copayments to patients, and concern whether the health benefits gained warrant the high cost (Danzon and Taylor 2010). Patients with higher OOP expenses are less likely to adhere to recommended treatment regimens, which may have a detrimental impact on health and recovery outcomes (President's Cancer Panel 2018). These financial burdens on patient and caregiver and their consequences are briefly discussed below.

3.1.1 Financial Toxicity

The increased costs of cancer care are negatively impacting patients and their families. Carrera et al (2018) define the nature of financial toxicity as the objective financial burden (arising from drug cost, other direct medical costs related treatment costs) and subjective financial distress of patients with cancer (such as anxiety and discomfort, wage loss, assets depletion) as a result of treatments using innovative drugs and concomitant health services. Financial toxicity is, thus, as a composite of objective financial burden and subjective financial stress among patients with cancer undergoing treatment, particularly as it relates to the newer classes of drugs. People with cancer are at higher risk for bankruptcy than people without a cancer diagnosis (Ramsey et al., 2013).

Among cancer patients in the United States, it is estimated that between 40 percent and 85 percent stop working during initial treatment, which can impose severe financial burden during the period of treatment (Ramsey et al 2013). Even for cancer patients with medical insurance, deductibles and co-payments for cancer treatments, supportive care and related services, along with nonmedical costs such as child care and lost income, may be financially devastating (Ramsey et al 2013). A national survey of cancer patients and their family members (by Kaiser Family Foundation 2006) showed that among those with insurance, 25% reported that they used all or most of their savings dealing with cancer, and 33% of families reported a problem paying their cancer care bills (Schnipper and Bastian 2016). Under health insurance schemes, newly diagnosed cancer patients often experience their highest OOP costs in the first two to three months following a positive screening or diagnosis until they meet their applicable deductible and out-of-pocket maximums (American Cancer Society Cancer Action Network 2017). Even, health insurance does not eliminate financial distress, out-of-pocket expenses and health disparities among cancer patients (Zafar et al 2013). One adverse outcome of financial toxicity is the abandonment, delay, and discontinuation of treatment (Carrera et al 2018). This results in a treatment gap.

3.1.2 Financial Hardship and Treatment Gap

Good-quality cancer care depends on the ability to secure, travel to and pay for needed diagnostics, treatments and support services (Cancer Support Community 2016). With skyrocketing prices of drugs, cancer treatment is becoming unaffordable and unsustainable. It is reported that in the United States, patients' health insurance status is a factor influencing an individual's ability to access high-quality cancer care (IOM 2013). People who do not have adequate health insurance or insurance coverage gap, or do not have savings or other financial resources, may forsake the treatment. The national survey by Kaiser Family Foundation (2006)[27] showed that among those individuals who were ever uninsured, 27% reported that they or their family member delayed or decided not to obtain care for cancer because of the cost. The 'President's Cancer Panel' report (2018), commenting on the affordability and access to lifesaving drugs, reflected that "when financial resources are strained, patients are less likely to follow treatment regimens, potentially worsening health outcomes these drugs are intended to improve." In the United States, studies have found that people associated with minority race/ethnicity and unemployment or underemployment face barriers to care, including insurance/financial concerns, a lack of social support and problems communicating with healthcare providers (Hendren et al 2011). In a U.S. survey of 1218 people (with 1,046 respondents), Cancer Support Community (2016) found that 22% of respondents reported skipping their recommended treatment to manage OOP costs in 2016. In a cohort US study, it has been estimated that "Overall, 20% took less than the prescribed amount of medication, 19% filled only part of a prescription, and 24% avoided filling prescriptions at all. A smaller portion of patients avoided procedures (7%) or tests (9%) because of costs. Seven percent spread out chemotherapy or clinic appointments, and 4% skipped appointments to save money" (Zafar et al 2013, P 383).

Although the continuing advancements in early detection, prevention, and treatment, is resulting in a steady increase in the number of cancer survivors, evidence also shows that many survivors face long-term health barriers to working for years after treatment. Fenn (2018) in a survey of 2108 patients, found that increased financial burden as a result of cancer care costs has been the strongest independent predictor of poor quality of life among cancer survivors. Many LMICs have not included cancer treatment in national health insurance coverage, nor do they have developed health insurance infrastructure, with the consequence that people not in regular employment or informal sector forfeit their treatment.

Commenting on system wide effect of the cost burden of cancer care, a 2013 Institute of Medicine study has cautioned that from a 'system perspective, health care costs, including the costs of cancer care, are on an unsustainable trajectory that could pose serious fiscal consequences for the United States'. In the United Kingdom (UK), the Cancer Drugs Fund– set up in 2011 to plug gaps in National Health Service funding for cancer drugs –overspent its allocated budget by 35% between 2013 and 2015; ballooning into a fund that, over its lifetime, cost £1.27 billion (Cancer Research UK 2016).In many countries, "vulnerable and underserved" people (people with lower socio-economic status) have difficulty accessing high-quality and timely cancer care.

4. Restraining Escalating Cost: The Proposals of Value Based Pricing, Competition Reforms and Introduction of Innovation Prizes

Healthcare markets in general, especially pharmaceutical markets, function less well than other sectors to align value, price, and cost, because necessary conditions of competitive market pricing are nearly (Danzon and Taylor 2010). Evidence shows that the price of cancer medicines is not aligned with the value of the medicine to the patient; rather patent-protected pharmaceutical companies set prices of new drugs at the highest level the 'market will bear' (Kantarjian et al 2014). For the United States, it is noted that cancer drug prices vary widely in different geographic regions, which supports the notion that drug prices reflect geopolitical and socioeconomics dynamics unrelated to the cost of drug development (see report by Experts in Chronic Myeloid Leukemia 2013). Competitive market conditions are infringed due to well-known factors, such as patents and other market exclusive rights that limit competition, lack of good information among patients, payers, and even physicians about the product characteristics (e.g., effectiveness and risks for new drugs), price insensitive demand, and wedge between the OOP prices consumers pay and the prices manufacturers receive, with the difference paid by insurance (Danzon and Taylor 2009). Patent-based monopoly pricing results in prices over which third-party payers and patients have limited negotiating power.

Citing data from the American Medical Association, the WHO report (2018) adds that drug companies make $14.50 on every $1 they spend on research and development for cancer drugs After the patents expire, collusive behavior among drug companies can tacitly maintain high prices over extended periods of time, despite competitive markets, thus representing a form of "collective monopoly (Experts in Chronic Myeloid Leukemia 2013).

Under the present system of less competitive markets, resources are being frittered in developing "Me too" drugs[28] for the market that offer no additional therapeutic benefits over the existing drugs in terms of extra life year gained or improvement in quality of life, despite carrying higher price tag. Evidence indicates that many highly priced new drugs lack meaningful synchronicity with benefits or outcomes in terms of additional years of life gained. For many tumors, drug prices do not reflect benefits of increased years and or improved quality of life (report by Experts in Chronic Myeloid Leukemia 2013). Of the 68 cancer drug indications approved by the European Medicines Agency (EMA) during 2009-13, 57% entered the market without evidence of a survival or quality of life benefit (Cohen 2017). The study by Kumar, Fojo and Mailankody revealed that only 19% of recently approved cancer drugs met the American Society of Clinical Oncology's goals for producing clinically meaningful survival outcomes for patients, despite often setting prices at extraordinarily high level. (The WHO 2018, Report) found that cancer drug research and development costs "may bear little or no relationship to how pharmaceutical companies set prices of cancer medicines." As per this report, evidence on pricing indicates that pharmaceutical companies, instead of setting prices according to the value of medicines, often place more emphasis on setting prices according to their income expectations.

It is suggested that prices of medicines and vaccine need to be aligned to three basic processes—innovation, incentive, and access—so that they become mutually reinforcing (Nathan 2007). A reasonable drug price should maintain healthy pharmaceutical company profits without being viewed as "profiteering" (making profit by unethical methods, like raising commodity prices after natural disasters) (Experts in Chronic Myeloid Leukemia 2013). Moreover, drug prices need to reflect value to the patients, that is, prices should be proportional to the benefit to patients in objective measures, such as survival prolongation, degree of tumor shrinkage, or improved quality of life (see report by Experts in Chronic Myeloid Leukemia 2013). On account of market imperfections, drug prices require normalizing by their respective expected health outcomes. The most widely accepted outcomes-adjusted price metric is the cost per (cost/ quality adjusted life year gained).[29] The European Society for Medical Oncology along with American Society of Clinical Oncology have released a compatible value framework to assess the value of cancer therapies (President's Cancer Panel; 2018 March). Developing and implementing a widely accepted value framework for cancer drugs is a critical step toward value-based pharmaceutical pricing (President's Cancer Panel; 2018 March).

4.1 Value Based Pricing

New generation of novel drugs and escalating costs of care have led many professional organizations to propose a new framework of measuring and/or ranking the value of novel interventions. Some of these new pricing frameworks (such as value-based pricing model) use the components of a cost-effectiveness analysis (CEA) (Mandelblatt,et al 2017). Cost-effectiveness analysis is a threshold-based value added pricing application, which uses the most widely accepted outcomes-adjusted price metric is the cost per quality-adjusted life year gained (cost/QALY). Comparison of cost/QALY provides a reasonable measure of the value gained per dollar spent across different drugs or health interventions, provided a standardized and comprehensive methodology is used to measure costs and outcomes (Dazon and Taylor 2009). Under this valued based pricing, higher prices are paid for drugs showing better treatment outcomes- not just outcome, but outcome per dollar spent (IOM 2014). To align drug prices with the drug's therapeutic value, Jaidev and Stiglitz (2009) have suggested replacing existing price-regulatory structures with a value-based approach to pricing. The American College of Physicians has called for this type of analysis to be a component of comparative effectiveness clinical research (Kirschner et al., 2008; Garber, 2008).

An alternative to Cost-effectiveness approach, it is suggested to make decision through comparative effectiveness research (CER). In a comparative effectiveness approach, the focus is more on clinical outcomes (e.g., safety) than on cost. Resource allocation can become less effective when large costs are associated with modest increases in health outcomes (Chandra et al., 2011). CER (comparative effectiveness research) is an analysis that takes into account cost-effectiveness data relative to clinical effectiveness in the setting of routine clinical practice. Emphasizing the need to consider the cost aspect along with comparative effectiveness research, Chandra et al. (2011, P13) state that, "comparative effectiveness research and its half-sibling cost-effectiveness research will provide a solid foundation for reform, once politicians and voters understand how dismal the alternative is." Some economists have argued in favor of a role for value-based pricing that rewards true pharmaceutical innovation so as to maintain incentives for pharmaceutical industry R&D, while keeping drug costs for consumers as reasonable as possible (Husereau & Cameron, 2011). A value-based system determines initial drug prices that consider cost-effectiveness data. Value-based pricing has been suggested as a method to improve the affordability of cancer therapy (Sullivan et al., 2011). In several countries, cost-effectiveness analyses are used to understand the economic value of a new technology and then to guide coverage decisions. A cost-effectiveness study uses an economic model to understand the amount of money required to provide an additional health benefit (Cressman et al 2015). The results are provided in the form of an incremental cost-effectiveness ratio, and one can understand the money needed to gain one quality-adjusted life year (QALY). For example, the drug bevacizumab was estimated to cost $571,000 per QALY in the first-line management of metastatic colorectal cancer in the United States (Goldstein et al 2017). Governments or insurance companies can then use the results of such studies to understand the cost-effectiveness of the technology and subsequently make decisions regarding coverage.

Assessing Cost-Effectiveness

The primary measurement tool in cost-effectiveness is the ICER—the ratio of the incremental cost of a new intervention versus the standard of care (the numerator) over the incremental health benefits (the denominator) (Garrison, 2010; Sullivan et al., 2011). The denominator is measured by the QALY or "utility." The metric, cost per QALY gained, and a threshold (expressed per QALY) can be considered a basis for "value-based pricing" and reimbursement.

A health intervention is considered to be cost-effective if ICER ($\Delta C/\Delta E$) relating to new drug minus the threshold ICER is zero or negative, where

$$\text{ICER} = \frac{Cost_{NewDrug} - Cost_{Comparator}}{Benefit_{NewDrug} - Benefit_{Comparator}} = \frac{\Delta C}{\Delta E} \qquad (1)$$

In UK NICE (National Institute for Health and Care Excellence) was established in 1999 to provide guidance to the NHS on whether new treatments and services are a cost-effective use of NHS budgets. To be deemed cost-effective, new drugs should normally cost no more than £20,000-£30,000 per QALY gained (Cancer Research UK 2016).

Use of Cost-Effectiveness in Canada, U.S and UK.

In Canada, the clinical effectiveness and cost-effectiveness of a drug is evaluated through the pan-Canadian Oncology Drug Review. There is no official ICER threshold in Canada; however, in the approval process the probability of rejection increases quickly above $50,000/QALY, and rejection is almost certain above $70,000/QALY. The threshold for oncology drugs and drugs for rare diseases is higher. However, most Canadian Drug Review recommendations do not reference an ICER threshold (Palmer, 2013).

Rocchi, Menon, Verma, and Miller (2008) suggest that the ICER is somewhat higher for accepting cancer therapies in Canada. Some expensive new medications which have not met cost-effectiveness benchmarks, and even the drugs that have demonstrated survival benefits and been endorsed in rigorous evidence-based guidelines, have not been funded by some Canadian provinces (see examples in Berry et al., 2012).

In the United States, healthcare reform has led to both heavy investment in CER(Cost Effectiveness Research) and the creation of a new regulatory framework for the oversight of the research. To improve evidence about the comparative effectiveness of alternative treatments, the U.S. Congress appropriated $1.1 billion toward acceleration of CER as part of the American Recovery and Reinvestment Act of 2009, where $1.1 billion was allocated as a "down payment" to support CER.

4.2 Stimulating and Maintaining Competition

The increasing cost of prescription drugs has become a source of concern for patients, prescribers, payers, and policy makers. Kesselheim et al (2016) have listed the following short-term strategies to address high prices in the context of the U.S. pharmaceutical market: enforcing more stringent requirements for the award and extension of exclusivity rights; enhancing competition by ensuring timely generic drug availability; providing greater opportunities for meaningful price negotiation by governmental payers; generating more evidence about comparative cost-effectiveness of therapeutic alternatives; and more effectively educating patients, prescribers, payers, and policy makers about these choices.

The most often suggested method to slow down the escalating prices of patented and branded products is to encourage the production of generics and biosimilars to biologic products. In the United States it is estimated that brand-name drugs accounted for 72% of drug spending between 2008 and 2015, and the prices for the most commonly used brand-name drugs increased 164% during that time period, far in excess of the consumer price index (12%)(Kesselheim et al (2016).

Promoting Generics and Bio-similar

Generic price competition is viewed as an important way to contain prices and increase patients' access to prescription medications. In the United States, the use of generics has increased since the initial enactment of the Drug Price Competition and Patent Term Restoration Act (HatchWaxman Amendments) in 1984. Generic oncology drugs are versions of brand name non-biological oncology drugs that are comparable in dosage, form, strength, route of administration, quality and performance characteristics, and intended use (Yang et al 2016).

Today, generic drugs account for 63% of all U.S. prescriptions for drugs (Frank 2007). The use of generics and biosimilars in oncology is growing exponentially, especially because of their lower costs (Yang et al 2016).

The evidence from different countries shows that despite the uptake of generics in the drug markets, the observed decrease in list price of generic entrants has been much smaller than expected (Cole, Sanoff and Dusetzina 2017)). In reality, practices and tactics such as product hopping, evergreening, and pay for delay can stand in the way of fair competition and fair prices. 'Product hopping'[30] or product switching occurs when brand name pharmaceutical companies introduce reformulations of their branded product that offer little or no therapeutic advantage. 'Evergreening' occurs when brand name companies patent as new drugs slight modifications of old drugs. 'Pay for delay' is a legal tactic in which branded drug manufacturers slow or obstruct generic competition by paying companies not to introduce lower-cost alternatives to the marketplace. Numerous examples show how pay-for-delay settlements have increased costs to consumers by billions of dollars in the United States

(Jones et al 2016). Angell (2004), commenting on the unethical practices of drug industry, mentions that the industry has been facing a wave of government investigations and civil and criminal lawsuits, such as "illegally overcharging Medicaid and Medicare, paying kickbacks to doctors, engaging in anti-competitive practices, colluding with generic companies to keep generic drugs off the market, illegally promoting drugs for unapproved uses, engaging in misleading direct-to-consumer advertising, and, of course, covering up evidence." There are also safety concerns for generic oncology products consumed in developing countries with less stringent manufacturing and supply chain regulations (Yang et al 2016).

Expensive biologics[31], while important treatments for a number of cancers, are significant drivers of escalating costs of cancer drugs. Biologics are large-molecule drugs produced in living organisms and are used to treat some of the most serious life-threatening diseases (Blackstone & Fuhr 2012). Biosimilars[32] have the potential to offer cost-savings with comparable efficacy and safety to innovator products. "The great economic advantage of biosimilars is that a manufacturer only needs to recreate the idea that has already been shown to work (Blackstone & Fuhr 2012)." Biosimilars are not "generic" versions of currently approved biologics, but instead, a biosimilar is a biologic drug that is highly similar (i.e., the two drugs have the same drug target, mechanism of action, and primary structure among other molecular similarities) to an approved reference biologic drug (originally patented drug or innovator product) (Henry and Taylor 2014). The American College of Physicians has endorsed the development of biosimilars in opposition to "extending market or data exclusivity periods beyond the current exclusivities granted to small-molecule, generic, orphan, and biologic drugs" (American Society of Clinical Oncology 2018). In Europe, nearly 30 biosimilars have been approved since 2006 (The President's Cancer Panel 2018). In the United States, the first two biosimilars for the treatment of cancer—one for bevacizumab (Avastin) and one for trastuzumab (Herceptin)—were recently approved, and others are under development (The President's Cancer Panel 2018).

4.3 Delinking Drug Prices from R&D Costs: Patents and Prizes Debate

Boldrine and Levine (2013) exploring the relationship between government-operated patent systems innovation and productivity, have suggest on the basis of both theory and evidence that while patents can have a partial equilibrium effect of improving incentives to invent, the general equilibrium effect on innovation can be negative. From the productivity angle (efficiency and value effectiveness), the current system is not working well. As Grootendorst et al (2011) point out that the most notable current feature of pharmaceutical innovation is the huge "drought" in the development of new products. In view of the various objections against patents and use of monopoly pricing practices(as discussed later), Kremer and Williams (2009), have argued have argued that if government intervention is indeed needed in pharmaceutical market, "a system of prizes might be superior to the existing system of monopolies"(cited by Boldrin and Levine 2013)[33]. Research prize is simply a transfer to the innovator for development of a particular invention. Several research studies suggest that prize awards can be a powerful mechanism for accelerating technological development (Brunt, Lerner & Nicholas 2011). According to Brunt et al, given the imperfections associated with patents, the literature on innovation incentives has attempted to evaluate the use of alternative, or complementary, mechanisms such as prizes.

The current patent system has come under widespread criticism on the grounds of inaccessibility to life-saving medicines to over 80% of the world population living in LMICs. For these countries, patents can impede medical care by pricing medicines and other health care technologies out of the reach of patients or their healthcare systems (Orbinski, Logan, and N-Marandi in Gold et al. 2009). Policy makers are trying to find a balance between promoting and rewarding innovation, ensuring access to medicines, and sustaining the viability of health systems (OECD 2018). One promising solution to meet the needs of the majority of the world's population and make cancer medicine available at affordable prices is to delink the financing of R&D from the pricing of end products so that medicines can be sold near the cost of production (Love 2012).To delink drug prices from R&D cost, researchers have put forward several proposals. One proposal is to institute cash prizes rather than patents to incentivize research. As discussed earlier, Love and Hubbard (2007) proposed to establish a fund that would reward successful developers of new products. Stiglitz and Jaidev (2010) have suggested "innovation Prizes"-a substantial onetime payment based on development cost incurred and the therapeutic value of novel medicine. Several other proposals for large medical prize funds have emerged, including the U.S. Medical Innovation Prize Fund, the

Bangladesh, Bolivia, and Suriname cancer prizes (as a reward mechanism for new cancer treatments and vaccines in developing countries), the Hollis/Pogge Health Impact Fund, and the proposal for a European cancer prize fund. According to the proposal for cancer funds in developing countries, it is suggested that these countries would place a percentage of cancer treatment budget towards a new prize for innovation. A country would then allocate more money for innovation prize awards proportionally as expenditures on treatment rise. Hollis and Pogg (2008) have suggested a staged approach-a variation of "Innovation Prizes" – in which periodic payments adjustments-in addition to the base payment, could be made in cases where there is considerable uncertainty around the therapeutic of new medicines. Grootendorst et al (2011) suggest the creation of "The Health Impact Fund" as an optional pay-for-performance scheme that would operate alongside the patent system. Lump-sum rewards for the new drugs[34], including proposals for prize funds underscore the need to reform the economic incentives of R&D for larger impacts on public health, to treat medicines as a public good, and to acknowledge the human rights to health (Quigley, 2015).

5. Meeting the Economic Challenge of Declining R&D Productivity

The issue of R&D productivity[35] has received increased attention since the late 1990s due to exponential growth in pharmaceutical R&D expenses and a decrease in the output of 'New Chemical Entities' (Paul et al., 2010). As Paul and colleagues maintain that without "a dramatic increase in R&D productivity, today's pharmaceutical industry cannot sustain sufficient innovation to replace the loss of revenues due to patent expirations for successful products" (P203). The drug development cost is driven by the high rate of clinical failure (Woodcock & Woosley 2008). Drug attrition rates for cancer are much higher than in other therapeutic areas (Hutchinson & Kirk, 2011). The success rate for new oncology drugs, from Phase I trials to U.S. approval by the Food and Drug Administration (FDA) in the period from 2003 to 2011, was around 6.7%—a figure that is about half the rate for non-oncological drugs (Hay, Thomas, Craighead, Economides, & Rosenthal, 2014; Thomas 2012; Moreno & Pearson 2013). The mean development time for antineoplastic drugs, from the time of application to NDA/BLA approval[36], is estimated to be 8.3 years (Kaitin & DiMasi, 2011).

Measuring R&D Productivity in Pharmaceuticals

As mentioned by Paul et al (2010), "R&D productivity can be viewed as an aggregate representation of both the efficiency and effectiveness of the drug discovery and development process; the goal of a highly productive R&D system is to efficiently translate inputs into the most desired and valuable outputs"(P204). Measuring R&D productivity[37] is a difficult task since the input builds are comprised of heterogeneous and multiple sources of knowledge. The output contains knowledge spill-overs that might last for several years, and the available data may not take into account the quality of the new molecular entity (NME). The 'pharmaceutical value equation' (Paul et al 2010, P 204) can be expressed as follows:

$$P \alpha \frac{WIP \times p(\mathrm{TS}) \times V}{CT \times \mathrm{C}} \qquad (1)$$

Where, *WIP*: the work in process; P: R&D productivity; *p*(TS): the probability of technical success; *V*: Value.

WIP (Work in Process) is the number of molecules in the drug discovery pipeline needed at each stage of development to achieve one NME launch. The probability of success per stage, *p*(TS), can be used to define the attrition rate as (1- *p*(TS). Attrition is considered as the likelihood of a project failing to advance to the next stage in the pipeline. It is estimated that about 11% of the molecules that enter pre-clinical development stage actually reach the market. For any given level of R&D investment, substantially reducing the total time from initial target to selection to commercial launch – or cycle time *(CT)*, or lowering costs *(C)* would increase productivity *(P)*. Value in healthcare (V), has been defined as health outcomes achieved per dollar spent (Porter, 2009). Many organizations across Europe measure value as societal gains, which involve estimating the duration of additional life with a new medicine, compared with that offered by standard therapy combined with an assessment of the quality of the life gained (Sullivan et al., 2011).

Following the literature, we can interpret the above equation in terms of two integral components in the productivity equation: R&D efficiency and R&D effectiveness, expressed as follows:

R&D productivity = R&D efficiency x R&D effectiveness

= (New products / R&D costs) x (Value / New products)

R&D efficiency = New products / R&D costs; and R&D effectiveness = Value / New products

The goal of a highly productive R&D system is to efficiently translate inputs into the most desired and valuable outputs (Paul et al., 2010). Following Paul et al., we can analyze R&D productivity by explaining its two dimensions: R&D efficiency and R&D effectiveness. R&D efficiency is the inverse of the ratio of inputs (ideas, investments, time, and money) to outputs (number of projects in pipeline, products launched), whereas R&D effectiveness is the ability of the R&D system to produce outputs with certain desired qualities (e.g., therapeutic value to patients and substantial commercial value)(see figure 1"Dimensions of R&D productivity" in Paul et al 2010).

Reversing the downward trends in R&D productivity can effectively offset cost escalations. As outlined above, R&D productivity is a combination of R&D efficiency and R&D effectiveness. Figure 1(in the text) presents a synoptic view of the efficient and cost-effective model of drug development process. The following subsections discuss these two aspects of R&D productivity.

5.1 R&D Efficiency

R&D efficiency in simple terms is expressed as the number of NMEs (New Molecular Entities) approved per billion US dollars spent on R&D. R&D efficiency at an organizational level results from the optimal use of technological and medical advances in the development of new drugs. Low productive efficiency is reflected in high attrition rates of drug development, and a slow, risky, and expensive R&D process. Reducing the attrition rate of drug candidates in clinical development represents the greatest challenge and opportunity for pharmaceutical R&D productivity (Paul et al 20010).

Accelerating R&D Efficiency

The current process of drug development involves more than a decade of gathering the necessary evidence to approve a new cancer drug and results in a low success rate whereby 60%–70% of late-stage cancer trials fail (de Lartigue, 2014; Menis, Hasan, & Besse, 2014).

As demonstrated in 7, oncology is the leading therapeutic area for late-stage failures. The high failure rate of oncology drugs after entering Phase III contributes to the higher average development costs in this area. Thomas (2012) found that from 2004 to 2011, the overall rate of transition from Phase I to FDA approval was 6.7% for oncology, while it was 12.1% for all other therapeutic areas. As few as 45% of oncology therapeutics progress from Phase III to NDA/BLA approvals, versus 64% for all other areas.

Table 7. Attrition Rates in Phase III Trials 2011–2012

Therapeutic Area	Failure Rate
Oncology	30%
Central Nervous System	14%
Musculoskeletal	8.5%
Infectious Diseases	29.50%
Cardiovascular	8.5%
Other	9.5%

Source: Arrowsmith and Miller, (2013)

Studies show that drug candidates failed in clinical trials due to a lack of efficacy, often because: the underlying clinical hypothesis about how to treat the disease was incorrect, there were unpredicted safety issues, or there were a greater proportion of drugs with novel mechanisms of action entering clinical trials without adequate proof-of-concept studies in humans (President's Council of Advisors on Science and Technology, 2012). Critics also assert that conventional randomized trials mask the benefits of drugs that only work in a subset of patients (Eisenstein, 2014). To address declining efficiency, researchers have proposed several measures to modernize the existing drug development process.

Modernizing the Drug Development Process and Incorporating Recent Scientific Advances

High attrition rates in late-phase clinical trials coupled with new opportunities unfolded by scientific advances in bio-sciences have challenged the traditional drug development process. In order to speed up the success rates, it will be necessary to reform clinical trials methodology, foster new models of collaborative and multidisciplinary research, and use advances in cancer genomics, computational biology, and bioinformatics.

Preventing Attrition Rates in Late-Phase Clinical Trials

One explanation for high drug prices and falling R&D productivity is that too many resources are often applied to the late-stage development of drug candidates with relatively low probability of success per stage, and/or post-launch support of marketed products (Paul et al., 2010; Pammoli, Magazzini, & Riccaboni, 2011). Phase III trials account for more than two-thirds of the cost of the clinical trials process. The reasons behind the attrition rate are clinical safety, toxicology, and lack of efficacy account for as much as 70% of failures in the clinic (Edwards 2008). Paul et al (2010) from their in-depth analysis of the pharmaceutical sector suggest that funding (operating R&D expenses) to early stage (Phase I and II) compounds are more beneficial in reducing attrition rates in the later stages (Phase ii, and phase iii). DiMasi and Grabowski (2007) suggest that greater investment in gathering relevant information in Phase I and Phase II trials can help increase oncology drugs success in Phase III clinical trials. A major challenge in drug development is the design of Phase II trials that more accurately predict success in Phase III trials. Paul et al suggest better target selection (selection of more validated and druggable targets). Another recommendation is to employ biomarkers and surrogate endpoints especially in phase 1(Paul et al 2010). In their emphasis on reducing attrition rates at later stages, Paul et al recommend "The quick win, fast fail drug development paradigm" (P212), using early POC (Proof of Concept) studies. In nutshell, as "the pharmaceutical industry transitions from an era of 'me-too' or 'slightly me-better' drugs to one of highly innovative medicines that result in markedly improved health outcomes, the pharmaceutical industry needs to re-focus its resources (money and talent) on discovery research and early translational medicine"(Paul et al 2010, P 213).

Knowledge gained from genomic research is beginning to be used to reform how clinical trials need to be designed and conducted (Reuben, Milliken, & Paradis, 2012). From the perspective of increasing efficiency, clinical trial methodologies need to achieve the following goals: (i) match drugs more effectively to the populations most likely to benefit based on an individual patient's molecular profile; (ii) develop adaptive trial designs that decrease trial costs by reducing the number of patients needed; and (iii) decrease the time from beginning drug trials to approval(American Association for Cancer Research, 2014; Carter, 2014). Each of these are discussed below.

Preventing Attrition Rates in Late-Phase Clinical Trials

One explanation for high drug prices and falling R&D productivity is that too many resources are often applied to the late-stage development of drug candidates with relatively low probability of success per stage, and/or post-launch support of marketed products (Paul et al., 2010; Pammoli, Magazzini, & Riccaboni, 2011). Phase III trials account for more than two-thirds of the cost of the clinical trials process. The reasons behind the attrition rate are clinical safety, toxicology, and lack of efficacy account for as much as 70% of failures in the clinic (Edwards 2008). Paul et al (2010) from their in-depth analysis of the pharmaceutical sector suggest that funding (operating R&D expenses) to early stage (Phase I and II) compounds are more beneficial in reducing attrition rates in the later stages (Phase ii, and phase iii). DiMasi and Grabowski (2007) suggest that greater investment in gathering relevant information in Phase I and Phase II trials can help increase oncology drugs success in Phase III clinical trials. A major challenge in drug development is the design of Phase II trials that more accurately predict success in Phase III trials. Paul et al suggest better target selection (selection of more validated and druggable targets). Another recommendation is to employ biomarkers and surrogate endpoints especially in phase 1(Paul et al 2010). In their emphasis on reducing attrition rates at later stages, Paul et al recommend "The quick win, fast fail drug development paradigm" (P212), using early POC (Proof of Concept) studies. In nutshell, as "the pharmaceutical industry transitions from an era of 'me-too' or 'slightly me-better' drugs to one of highly innovative medicines that result in markedly improved health outcomes, the pharmaceutical industry needs to re-focus its resources (money and talent) on discovery research and early translational medicine"(Paul et al 2010, P 213).

Knowledge gained from genomic research is beginning to be used to reform how clinical trials need to be designed and conducted (Reuben, Milliken, & Paradis, 2012). From the perspective of increasing efficiency, clinical trial methodologies need to achieve the following goals: (i) match drugs more effectively to the populations most likely to benefit based on an individual patient's molecular profile; (ii) develop adaptive trial designs that decrease trial costs by reducing the number of patients needed; and (iii) decrease the time from beginning drug trials to approval(American Association for Cancer Research, 2014; Carter, 2014). Each of these are discussed below.

Providing the Right Treatment to the Right Patient at the Right Dose at the Right Time

Biomarkers and individualized molecular medicine are replacing traditional "one size fits all" medicine. Every person has a unique variation of the human genome, the knowledge of which can be leveraged to provide sophisticated personalized medicine. Genetic testing of patients and cancer, along with biomarker-based diagnostic testing, have increased the potential for identification of patient subgroups with the greatest probability of achieving clinical benefit from particular drugs (Chin, Andersen, & Futreal, 2011). The use of genomics in clinical research allows for the use of novel clinical trial designs to assign the correct therapy to the correct patient earlier in the process, and to improve organ-based classifications of cancers by including a description of the underlying genomic alterations. New clinical trials driven by tumour biology with the incorporation of predictive and pharmacodynamic biomarkers might be beneficial in drug development (Moreno & Pearson 2013). New developments in genomics facilitate the prediction of which patients will likely have a tumor that is resistant to a certain therapy and to identify combinations of therapies that will overcome resistance (American Association for Cancer Research, 2014). In the pursuit of tailored therapeutics, Paul et al (2010) in their productivity analysis have endorsed the use of biomarkers to appropriately select patient subpopulations will also have a positive effect on p(TS) in the later stages of clinical development.

Pharmacogenetics tests under development are a means to improve the safety and efficacy of drug treatment. Pharmacogenomics (PGx)—the study of variations of DNA and RNA characteristics as related to drug response—is a critical area of personalized medicine where significant progress has recently been made (Simoncelli, 2013). The use of molecular diagnostics, including testing for genes, gene expression, proteins, and metabolites, is expected to provide greater efficiency, value, and cost savings when integrated into new cancer therapies as a bundled package (Kalia, 2013).

Personalized genomics plays a vital role (e.g., PGx) in the evolving model of personalized medicine. Personalized medicine uses traditional, as well as emerging, concepts of the genetic and environmental basis of disease to individualize disease prevention, diagnosis, and treatment (Offit, 2011). Recent studies have revealed extensive genetic diversity both between and within tumors. A major cause of genetic heterogeneity in cancer is genomic instability. These issues are hurdles to improving cancer treatment outcomes with novel molecularly targeted agents (Catenacci, 2015). Overcoming these hurdles as well as accelerating the pace of drug development so that appropriate therapies can be delivered quickly to suitable patients has resulted in adaptive designs becoming more popular in clinical trial and drug development. Unlike traditional trial designs, adaptive designs use accumulating data to modify the ongoing trial without undermining the integrity and validity of the trial (Zang & Lee, 2014). Driven by our increased understanding of the genetic mutations, master protocol design clinical trials, "basket" and "umbrella" trials have been developed to answer multiple questions within a single overall clinical trial (AACR 2018, figure 11, P55).[38] Basket and umbrella trial designs[39] are newer adaptive approaches to testing targeted therapeutics in oncology. These novel clinical trial designs address the challenges of both inter- and intra-patient tumor molecular heterogeneity. One basket trial that has led to an FDA approval for patients with a rare type of cancer characterized by a defined genetic mutation is highlighted in Molecularly Targeting Blood Cancers) AACR 2018 P 50).

In both **basket and umbrella trials**, the right therapeutics are matched with the right patients earlier in the process. This reduces the number of patients who need to be enrolled in the trial before it is determined whether or not the anticancer therapeutic being evaluated is safe and effective. If shown to be safe and effective, it can decrease the length of time it takes for a new anticancer therapeutic to be made available to patients (American Cancer Society 2018). In the basket trial one drug is tested against a particular genetic mutation, while in the umbrella trial different drugs are tested against multiple genetic mutations within a single histology (P50American Cancer Society 2018).[40] The following section elaborates on new adaptive trial designs.

Adaptive Trial Designs

An adaptive design is one in which the accumulating data is used to modify the trial's course (Berry, Evans, Strevel, & Bell, 2012); they "adapt" in response to information generated during the trial. Trial expenses can be reduced, and drug development efficiency increased using adaptive trial designs by enabling researchers to address multiple and changing hypotheses during the course of a single clinical trial (Alexander et al., 2013). Adaptive approaches make each research phase a learning tool to improve the next phase in a flexible process that can accelerate timelines, reduce costs, and generate the most knowledge from the smallest number of patients. In traditional trials, decisions regarding dosage, randomization, and sample size are made in advance and do not generally change throughout the study (Reitsma & Berry, 2013).

The Bayesian approach, an ideal tool for building adaptive designs (Berry, 2011) uses both evidence that accumulates over time (e.g., interim clinical trial data) and prior information (literature or previous relevant studies). This combination of evidence provides a "posterior distribution" (a term for the probability of an event that is conditional on the prior information and current data), which is analyzed to draw conclusions (National Pharmaceutical Council, 2012). Experimental arms are dropped early in Phase II if they fail to be effective in any subset of disease. Biomarker-based trials have numerous efficiencies, but the major efficiency is enabling a Phase III trial that is smaller than is traditionally needed, as in an adaptive trial including only patients who are most likely to respond in the study (American Association for Cancer Research, 2014; American Association for Cancer Research, 2011).

Both I-SPY 2 and BATTLE trials are examples of adaptive design clinical trials (Reuben et al., 2012; Kim et al., 2011). These novel trials are being deployed for faster testing of new drugs against particular molecular targets (Dizon et al., 2016). According to Alexander et al. (2013), "a wholly new paradigm for drug development exemplifying personalized medicine is evinced by an adaptive trial called I-SPY2, in which drugs from many companies are evaluated in the same trial—a Phase II screening process." A key feature of this trial design is the use of interim analyses, which permits researchers to customize the trial, for example, by adjusting the randomization process or treatment dose or schedule based on results from earlier participants in the study. That is, in

I-SPY 2 the success is measured in terms of predicting regulatory success in a future confirmatory phase III trial. These predictions use the Bayesian approach and are based on information currently available in the trial (Bates et al., 2015).

The promise of personalized ("precision") medicines and the rapid success resulting from drug repositioning for anticancer applications from non-cancer drugs offer substantial opportunities in transforming the prevailing time-consuming and costly drug discovery process into a more productive one in terms of time, cost, and efficacy.

Personalized Medicine & Drug Repositioning: Implications for Productivity of Current Drug Discovery Pipelines

As mentioned earlier, the traditional drug discovery process is observed to fail in clinical trials often because of toxicity or lack of efficacy and involves enormous time and cost to develop new drugs. Lack of efficacy in the conventional drug development occurs largely due to disease heterogeneity among patients. The discovery of the genetic underpinnings of cancer set the stage for the new era of precision/personalized medicine (AACR 2018). Personalized medicines, by stratifying patients and diseases into molecular subtypes and treating with subtype-specific drugs, help to address this failure and improve drug efficacy (Li & Jones, 2012). Personalized medicine diagnoses patients and prescribes drugs tailored to the molecular biology of the individual's disease. To increase the benefit (and reduce risks) of a drug treatment, or the value effectiveness, V[41], it is often important to aim to personalize or tailor the use of the therapy (Paul et al 2010).

Rapid advances in disease biology, genomics, and bioinformatics have also expanded the potential of drug repositioning for anticancer applications from non-cancer drugs. Drug repositioning refers to the identification of new indications from existing drugs and the application of the newly identified drugs to the treatment of diseases other than the drug's intended disease (Shim & Liu, 2014).

Given the considerable time and cost of developing new drugs, a much more efficient option is to reposition drugs from other disease indications when possible. Drug repositioning is considered an efficient approach to drug discovery, since reusing drugs that have previously passed clinical trials can be expected to minimize the risk of failure in future late-stage clinical trials due to toxicity, and thus would lead to faster drug approvals (Li & Jones, 2012). Li & Jones have provided a review of 46 approved drugs already repositioned for new therapeutic use. As most non-cancer drugs have little or tolerable side effects in humans, repositioning of non-cancer drugs for anticancer therapy can be an excellent strategy for future anticancer drug development (Shim & Liu, 2014).

Some studies have raised financial viability issues regarding the pricing and revenue generation of pharmaceutical companies in the landscape of stratified medicine, where smaller patient populations are treated individually in a personalized medicine approach. Trusheim, Berndt, & Douglas (2007) analyzed the economic and financial viability of stratified (personalized) medicine as compared to empiric medicine (a medicine prescribed to all patients with a particular condition using net present value analysis). The authors used a simulation exercise to demonstrate that with current incentive structures, the segmenting and sub-segmenting of a disease, under a stratified medicine system, can make therapeutic markets too small to be economically viable. Stratified medicine may not be economically viable without significant pricing and total oncology outlay flexibility by payers to encourage private sector investment in drug development for smaller cancer patient cohorts. The authors argue that policy tools such as accelerated approvals, adaptive licensing, and novel clinical trial designs appear to be the most promising methods to improve the economic incentives facing drug developers. In the next ten years, it has been estimated that personalized medicine will grow to 5%–10% of the entire pharmaceuticals market. Several companies have already established diagnostic divisions to identify new biomarkers and meet their related diagnostic needs in-house by combining drug development with the production of the related diagnostic test (Kalia, 2013).

Alternative Surrogate, Endpoints, and Expedited Review Programs for Oncology Drugs

In order to reduce the time needed for the trial to continue before a clear result can be achieved, two efforts are required. They include using alternative or surrogate endpoints[42] and the FDA's expedited review strategies (American Association for Cancer Research, 2014).

Traditionally, an improvement in overall survival has been considered the "gold standard"—the most convincing measure of efficacy. Given the number of active therapies for potential investigation, demand for rapid evaluation and early availability of new therapies is growing. The FDA requires cancer drug approval to be based on direct evidence of clinical benefit, using endpoints such as improvements in overall survival, health-related quality of life, tumor-related symptoms, and/or physical functioning. More recently, sophisticated monitoring of trial participants now provides alternative clinical benefit measures. Using these endpoints can decrease trial duration and required enrollment numbers, and also permit single arm trial design, which reduces cost. In an analysis of 14 clinical trials, the FDA identified strong correlations between response rates and progression-free survival endpoints in non-small cell lung cancer patients (Clarke, Wang, & Ready, 2015). The implication is that response rate could be used as an early surrogate endpoint for progression-free survival, reducing the time required for this clinical trial. Particular drug regimens may also offer opportunities for accelerated drug approval by the FDA. Recently the FDA announced that neoadjuvant trials for early breast cancer with high recurrence risk and unfavorable prognosis will be considered for accelerated drug approval, and the neoadjuvant pertuzumab was given accelerated approval in September 2013 (Bardia & Baselga, 2013).

New medical advances have reinforced the need for drug evaluations and approval procedures to align more closely with patient requirements for timely access to new technologies and data to inform medical decisions. To achieve the goal of expediting patient access to needed therapies, regulators, health technology assessment bodies, and payers around the world have been actively pursuing various approaches to ensure the timely availability of important medicines for patients in need. The following subsection deals with this effort.

There are four evidence-based strategies to expedite the assessment of therapeutics for life-threatening cancer, which are: (i) accelerated approval, (ii) fast track, (iii) breakthrough therapy, and (iv) priority review (American Association for Cancer Research, 2014). These programs complement one another and serve a common goal: to speed up the approval of effective treatments for serious conditions. However, the use of smaller trials in these programs to accelerate drug development increases potential for risk of bias, efficacy, and safety (Kluetz & Donoghue, 2014).

The UK launched a program called the "Early Access to Medicines Scheme" to speed up the development of new treatments in areas of high unmet medical need. The EMA started a pilot project in adaptive licensing, and the New Drug Development Paradigms Program at the Massachusetts Institute of Technology is working to determine what evidence is needed to support the development of new pathways. The EMA proposes an adaptive licensing approach, also referred to as staggered approval or progressive licensing, aimed at improving patient access to new therapeutics (Eichler et al., 2012). This differs from the FDA's accelerated approval approach, where products are granted a tentative approval for a broader indication based upon interim trial data. The adaptive licensing approach approves medications for a narrowly defined patient population, which is then iteratively broadened if followed by supporting evidence from these patients (Gaffney, 2014).

Restricting Intellectual Property Rights in Upstream Bio-Medical Research: Expanding Upstream Research in Public Domain

Promoting basic research through public funding is considered to be a cornerstone of translational research. The science that supports early drug discovery is funded mainly by governments and is conducted in academic or public-sector laboratories (Grootendorst et al 2011). Biomedical research comes from a tradition of open science- that is, the culture of upstream research. The "Open Science" or "science commons," or knowledge that is widely accessible at low or no cost, plays two important roles that proprietary R&D cannot: it enables practical benefits even in the absence of profitable markets for goods and services, and its lays a shared foundation for subsequent private R&D (Cook-Deegan 2006). It is primarily, although not exclusively, funded by government and nonprofit sources. Evidence shows that much development of Pharmaceuticals products is done outside the private sector than it is ordinarily imagined (Boldrin & Levine 2013). In the United States, the NIH spends more than half of its budget supporting basic research. NIH-funded basic research projects significantly contribute to novel target identification and drug development (American Cancer Society Report (ACSR) 2018). According to the American Cancer Society Report, the discovery of DNA and its 3-dimensional structure paved the way for understanding genetic mutations, the underlying basis of most cancers. Building on that, the report notes that decades of basic research in immunology led to the development of immunotherapies that have revolutionized the field of cancer treatment (ACSR 2018). Genomic biology is now a fundamental aspect of research strategies and is in the process of leading to the realization of "personalized medicine" (National Academies Press 2011, Burke, Trinidad and Press 203).

Markets fail to provide sufficient incentives for investment in research due to its non- appropriable character, and its risky and intangible nature. As a result, the private sector provides 'sub-optimal' levels of research investment and government support must ensure the provision of the basic research required for innovation and economic growth (OECD 2011). According to a report from the National Science Board US (2012), "Business sector investment focuses largely on development, directing almost 80% of its R&D resources toward development, compared to only 13.9% toward applied research and an estimated 5% towards basic research in 2009. Development funding generally supports incremental rather than transformative innovation" (P 3). This report further adds that "Transformative innovation is more likely when basic research leads to quantum steps in expanding knowledge or through synergies when progress in multiple areas of science or technology complement each other to provide new composite capabilities (P3)." In the United States, the Federal government plays a critical role, accounting for 53% of all U.S. basic research funding, compared to 22% for the business sector. In the European Union, 52% of the government's budget appropriation for R&D went to basic research in 2013 (UNESCO 2017). Strength in basic research is essential for any country that wishes to keep producing frontier technologies in rapidly evolving markets. Disciplines of molecular biology, biotechnology

and pharmaceuticals and nanotechnology are among the next waves of high technology areas (UNESCO 2017), warranting strong support from public R&D funding and public sponsored basic research.

Upstream Research and Downstream Product Development

The relationship between R&D and innovations is quite complex (NSB 2012). In most countries, including the United States, only a small number of businesses perform R&D. Under the commons model, the Federal government sponsored premarket or "upstream" research and encouraged broad dissemination of results in the public domain. Unpatented biomedical discoveries were freely incorporated in "downstream" products for diagnosing and treating disease. In cancer research, the basic research is conducted in academic or public-sector laboratories that often identifies cellular proteins (known as targets) implicated in disease pathways (Grootendorst, et al 2011). These authors argue that the present patent system rewards the commercial pharmaceutical companies for development of follow-on drugs. Boldrine and Levine(2013) have argued that the downstream social cost of monopoly pricing of pharmaceutical products has been found to the highest for life savings drugs and the cost of monopoly pricing of other pharmaceutical products has also been quite high. To illustrate their argument, these authors point out that under the current law, the chemical formula and the efficacy of the cure as established by clinical trials are made available to competitors essentially for free(P13). Corroborating the evidence from the drug development process, Boldrine and Levine mention that about 80 percent of the "initial cost of drug development comes from Stage III clinical trials, a public good that legislation requires be *privately* produced" (P13).

From a detailed study of human genome projects under both public and private agencies, Cook-Deegan (2006), exhorts that without an expansive science commons deliberate policy to promote open access and low-cost use, many benefits would be lost, and profit-driven private genomics would be vastly less productive and valuable.

Since 1980, biomedical research has, however, been moving from a commons model toward a privatization model (Heller & Eisenburg, 1998 a)[43] As mentioned by Angell (2004), the Bayh-Dole Act has enabled universities and small businesses to patent discoveries emanating from research sponsored by the National Institutes of Health (NIH), the major distributor of tax dollars for medical research, and then to grant exclusive licenses to drug companies. Over the past two decades in the United States, research institutions such as the NIH and major universities have created technology transfer offices to patent and license their discoveries (Heller & Eisenberg, 1998b). Heller et al further add that commercial biotechnology firms have emerged in R&D niches somewhere between the "fundamental" research of academic laboratories and the targeted product development of pharmaceutical firms. Privatization and intellectual property protection through patents hold both promises and risks. In markets where innovation is cumulative, the overall effectiveness of IP in promoting innovation also depends on how far IP rights on existing technologies hinder subsequent innovation (Williams 2013). In biosciences, innovation is cumulative in the sense that discoveries are inputs into follow-on discoveries, as a result of which privatization of biomedical research must be more carefully deployed to sustain both upstream research and downstream product development. But privatization can stifle research in downstream, when too many owners hold patent rights in prior discoveries in the upstream market.

The ongoing proliferation of intellectual property rights in biomedical research suggest a tragedy of "anti-commons," in which downstream firms under-use scarce resources because too many owners in the upstream market have a right to exclude others from a scarce resource (Heller & Eisenberg, 1998a). The current patent system is creating a "patent thicket"—an overlapping of rights requiring that those seeking to commercialize new technology obtain licenses from multiple patentees (Shapiro, 2001). When there are so many patents potentially held by different owners—and they may overlap in their protective scope—it's not clear who to contact to obtain all the necessary licenses. Wasteful underuse can, thus, arise when ownership rights and regulatory controls are too fragmented (Heller & Eisenberg, 2010).

The sequencing of the human genome provides a useful empirical context in examining the effects of Intellectual property (IP) for promoting or hindering subsequent innovations. Considering the case of human genome in particular, Williamsons (2013)s has found evidence that intellectual property (IP) rights on existing technologies hinder subsequent innovation. Using data on the sequencing of the human genome by the public Human Genome Project[44] and the private firm Celera, Williamsons (2013) estimated the impact of Celera's gene-level IP on subsequent scientific research and product development. William's paper found that Celera-held genes saw roughly 30 percent fewer scientific publications about genotype-phenotype links, and a similar decrease in availability of genetic tests. William's paper suggests that increasing the price of using already discovered knowledge, at least in gene research, decreases downstream product development, and significantly so. Analyzing various genome projects, both public and private, Cook-Deegan (2006) suggests the need to support open science and a healthy science common upon which both public and private science can draw. Cook-Deegan further contends that without explicit policies to foster the science commons, this valuable pool of knowledge would have been shallower, resulting in a less productive fountain of social benefits.

Expediting Translational Research through New Models of Collaborative and Multidisciplinary Research

The growing complexity and multidisciplinary nature of research in life sciences is creating an ever-increasing need for bridging the gap between basic advances in biosciences and their clinical applications. One manifestation of this gap is the lack of growth of new drug approvals, despite a more than 10-fold increase in inflation-adjusted spending by the pharmaceutical and biotechnology industries over the past 40 years (Coller & Califf, 2009). Addressing this gap is difficult because clinical and basic scientists don't really communicate (Butler, 2008). In Butler's view, the separation in the ecosystems of basic and clinical research has widened with the explosion of advances in molecular biology in the 1970s. As a result, the bulk of biomedical research is now conducted by highly specialized scientists who largely focus on publishing research in top journals, while physician-scientists are in the minority (Butler, 2008). The advances in genomics, proteomics and all its cousins are generating such a volume of potential drug targets and other discoveries that the pharmaceutical industry is having trouble digesting them (Butler, 2008). The NIH estimates that 80 to 90 percent of potential therapeutics in preclinical testing run into problems that preclude them from advancing to the clinical trial phase (Hobin et al., 2012). The gulf between finding a promising new agent and demonstrating its safety and efficacy in humans is termed as the "valley of death" (Coller & Califf, 2009). Bridging the chasm between "bench to bedside" requires the research model to be based on the closer working relationship among multidisciplinary groups including both basic scientists and clinical scientists, but also bioinformaticians, statisticians, engineers, and industry experts (Butler, 2008; Zerhouni, 2005). It is acknowledged that research questions may originate from clinical practice as well as from the laboratory so including a diverse group of professionals can augment the study.

To overcome the challenges of the translational gap, the United States has developed translational platforms such as the NIH Clinical Translational Science Awards program. Subsequent to the NIH actions and priorities, national and government agencies in European countries are according similar status and importance to translational research. The British Medical Research Council and the European Advanced Translational Research Infrastructure in Medicine have emerged as parallel institutions in translational research. Similarly, in 2011, the NIH proposed the creation of an important new entity, the National Center for Advancing Translational Sciences (NCATS), to serve as NIH's catalytic hub for translational innovation (Bonter, Desjardins, Currier, Pun, & Ashbury, 2011). NCATS was established with the aim of transforming the translational process so that new treatments and cures for disease can be delivered to patients faster.

There are expectations for a significant impact of fields in medicine, such as human genomics, transcriptomics, proteomics, and metabolomics leading to more effective personalized medical care and disease prevention in the near future (Khoury et al., 2007). These fields are rapidly developing potentially useful biomarkers; yet, clinical translation is currently challenging due to a number of factors. The most relevant are the imprecisely defined patient cohorts available for clinical trials, and a lack of standardization among protocols of specimen handling, collection, and storage (Vucic et al., 2012). However, the existing strengths of academia, biotechnology, and pharmaceutical companies are capable of complementing on another to address the challenges that limit drug discovery and development (Lengauer, Diaz, & Saha, 2005). The following sections deal with the public and private industry partnerships at the national level and research collaboration on an international scale.

Public-Private Partnership

It is argued that neither public sector nor the private sector alone may lack sufficient capability to meet the grand challenge of productivity growth. Public sector by funding 'unguided research' that can result transformative discoveries, and by conducting collaborative research with the private sector in areas of target validation, predictive toxicology etc. become a successful model of public private partnership (PPP) (Edwards 2008). Government R&D support and partnership with private industry for translational research plays a critical economic role, since it reduces technical and market risk sufficiently to encourage industry to invest the far larger funds required for applied R&D (Tassey, 2014). Public and private research partnerships combine knowledge, reduce potential conflicts of interest, and provide management specialties to maximize societal benefit of new technologies (Stiglitz & Jayadev, 2010). In view of the various beneficial spillover effects of public investment, Stiglitz and Jaidev(2011) recommend public funding of Phase III clinical trials and propose: (a) research cost-sharing among all stakeholders including industry, public, and nonprofit research institutions; (b) dissemination of research into the public domain; (c) partnerships for conducting research that utilize respective skills, facilitate technology transfer, and promote collective learning between academic and industrial scientists.

The critical areas where publicly funded clinical cancer research may be needed include opportunities to optimize treatment regimens for approved drugs or therapies, such as in adjuvant therapy, timing of multimodal therapies, optimal dosing and scheduling, and combination therapies that involve multiple industry sponsors (Bertagnolli, Canetta, & Nass, 2014). In the case of precision medicines, recruiting sufficient numbers of patients with particular cancer subtypes into clinical trials is challenging and requires collaborative efforts from research groups and industry to accelerate progress. Innovative trial designs such as the I-SPY and BATTLE trials, basket trials, and biomarker-enrichment designs are costly and require a large, well-trained research network (Bertagnolli et al., 2014).

In 2010, a committee appointed by the Institute of Medicine of the National Academy of Sciences called for more active engagement and better alignment of incentives among the cooperative groups in the U.S., including the National Cancer Institute of the NIH, the FDA, and the biopharmaceutical industry (Bertagnolli et al., 2014). Through its Clinical and Translational Sciences Award Program, the NIH funds centers to facilitate the translation of basic research findings into clinical applications (Hamburg & Collins, 2010). The NIH and the FDA have developed a collaboration between regulatory and translational science to accelerate the translation of research into medical products and therapies.

Collaboration between pharmaceutical companies, academic institutions, small and medium enterprises, patients, and regulatory authorities aimed at supporting drug development across Europe is exemplified by the Innovative Medicines Initiative, which launched in 2008 as a large-scale public-private partnership of the European Commission and the European Federation of Pharmaceutical Industries and Associations (Vaudano, 2013). As another example on the research side to accelerate the development of drugs to treat rare and neglected diseases, NIH's Therapeutics for Rare and Neglected Diseases Program exists in an open environment, which permits the involvement of all of the world's top experts on a given disease (Hamburg & Collins, 2010).

There is a need for increased sample sizes in clinical trials when investigations are aimed at examining evidence for a personalized medicine approach in order to sufficiently represent different patient sub-populations. Large clinical trials often require large collaborations on the national or international scale (Cancer Research UK, 2014). Collaboration on molecular screening platforms to best identify and enroll appropriate clinical trial candidates has been proposed by the European Organization for Research and Treatment of Cancer (EORTC) (Lacombe, 2014). This represents a new approach to high-quality integrated infrastructure for efficient screening of patients with specific molecular alterations. In the United States, the Translational Research Working Group was established in 2005 to work with the cancer research community to develop recommendations about how the NCI could best organize its efforts to further translational research.[45] Structures including practice-based research networks have been developed as a mechanism to move research into clinical practice. The structural genomics consortium (SGC) is another example of a successful public–private partnership (Edwards 2008)

Another important recent trend is a move toward open international research partnerships to speed up the drug discovery process. Paul et al (2010) suggests expanding the opportunities to partner virtually all elements of R&D through a coordinated and global network or FIPNet could (if effectively managed) substantially improve R&D productivity by affordably enhancing the pipeline from early discovery through to launch. The International Cancer Research Partnership is one example of international collaboration that includes cancer research funders from the United States, Canada, Europe, Japan, and Australia. The International Cancer Research Partnership is a unique alliance of cancer organizations working together to enhance global collaboration and strategic coordination of research. The group operates through regular teleconferences and annual face-to-face meetings, as well as publishing portfolio analyses and evaluation reports. Other examples include aligning national/regional translational cancer research programs and activities in translational cancer research and the International Rare Cancers Initiative, which partners with the EORTC, the NCI, and the International Cancer Genome Consortium. With rising drug discovery cost, the industry has been exploring avenues to get optimal value from R&D budget. Many large pharma companies and global contract research organizations (CROs) have set up or are trying to create research centers in China, India and Singapore, which offer breadth of preclinical and clinical services at significant savings of 30–80% versus the cost in the USA (Khanna 2012).

Open-access online data resources, open-source programming tools, and open-access peer-reviewed journals also help support these collaborative research efforts by providing bioinformatics tools and support for the large volume of data. For example, the cBio Cancer Genomics Portal[46] provides multidimensional cancer genomics data on 5,000 tumor samples from 20 cancer studies and was developed at the Memorial Sloan-Kettering Cancer Center to complement several existing data portals. The IntOGen-mutations platform identifies and visualizes cancer-driving mutations facilitating ranking of different mutations and potentially aiding clinical decision making (Cerami et al., 2012). Open-source programming tools are available at the Biopython project, a collaboration of volunteers that provide Python libraries for a wide range of bioinformatics analyses. Biopython includes modules for reading and writing different DNA and protein sequence file formats, working with 3D molecular models of drug target and other proteins, interacting with established online sequence tools, as well as modules for statistical learning (Cock et al., 2009). Bioconductor is another open source framework for bioinformatics and computational biology. The Public Library of Science (PLoS) publishes many open access journals including PLOS Computational Biology, which promotes open and unrestricted access to scientific publications, computational research tools and methods, as well as software.

Enhancing the Success Rate in the Future through Advances in Big Data, Computational Biology and Bioinformatics

Various technological advances in DNA sequencing have dramatically increased the number of known cancer-associated genomic alterations. The volume of data presents many bioinformatics challenges for statisticians and biologists including data acquisition, data management, data transformation, data modeling, and combining data from different sources. Genomics-driven big data (genotyping, gene expression, sequencing data) poses significant research and practical challenges (Chen, Chiang and Storey 2012). Recent advances in machine learning methods may also present opportunities for computational biology and bioinformatics (CBB) (Gentleman et al., 2004). Bioinformatics is an interdisciplinary field that combines computer science, statistics, mathematics, and engineering to analyze and interpret biological data. Computational biology is the science of using biological data to develop algorithms and assist in modeling biological systems. Cancer computational biology focuses on large-scale data to examine mutational trajectory of cancers and other processes playing a role in cancer. Large-scale datasets of millions of data points are made possible by high-throughput techniques utilizing robotics and large-scale automation (Yakhini & Jurisica, 2011).

The integration of large-scale omics data with epidemiological data from well-defined patient populations improves the statistical power to correlate genetic mutations with environmental influences and clinical pathology. Discovery of novel correlations has the potential to improve our understanding of specific cancers and provide more individualized disease management (Vucic et al., 2012). Enormous research efforts will be needed in the field of CBB in order to efficiently mine the huge amounts of information generated by the genomic analyses of tumors and to identify the genomic alterations most likely to yield therapeutic targets with the potential to benefit patients.

The pharmaceutical industry requires a shift in methodology to analyze drug data. Computational pharmacology is a methodological approach to discover links between genotypes and diseases, and then screening data for therapeutic drug candidates (Price, 2012). Ideally, large centralized shared databases will house sequence data from hundreds of thousands of tumors submitted by researchers (American Association for Cancer Research, 2014). Cloud solutions have become essential to genomics research because of the vast amount of data produced by researchers[47] and the difficulties inherent in transferring such large datasets between sites. Cloud computing eliminates the requirement for downloading data in order to work with it and greatly reduces the time required for bioinformatics investigations. To efficiently mine the enormous amounts of information generated by the genomic analyses of tumors, and to identify the genomic alterations most likely to yield therapeutic targets with the potential to benefit patients, biomedical researchers will need efficient algorithms to predict cancer-induced mutations found using whole-genome sequencing data. In addition to identifying the most promising therapeutic targets, CBB may help pinpoint the best combinations of therapeutics.

Researchers in biosciences need to engage with and learn from researchers across fields, including mathematics, engineering, and the physical, chemical, and social sciences. Converting information from multidimensional data sets to identify useful biomarkers for classification of tumor prognosis, tumor therapeutic response, and tumor therapeutic targets will require a cross-disciplinary systems biology approach (Gonzalez-Angulo, Hennessy, & Mills, 2010). Systems biology, utilizing high-throughput technologies to identify molecular drivers and biomarkers of cancer, integrates approaches of engineering, physics, and mathematics with biological and medical data. This approach aims to make clinical trials smaller, shorter, cheaper, and individualized while increasing trial efficiency. Achieving these aims will effectively hasten the evolution of personalized medicine (Gonzalez-Angulo, Hennessy, & Mills, 2010).

5.2 Improving R&D Effectiveness

In words of Paul et al (2010), "R&D effectiveness can be defined as the ability of the R&D system to produce outputs with certain intended and desired qualities (for example, medical value to patients, physicians and payers, and substantial commercial value P304). Analysts have expressed concerns about the relationship between the escalating drug prices and therapeutic quality of new medicines. There is a real innovation crisis stemming mostly from current incentives that reward companies for developing large numbers of new drugs with few clinical advantages over existing ones (Light & Lexchin, 2012). Evidence clearly indicates that the great majority of "new" drugs in the market are not new or innovative at all but merely variations of older drugs already on the market (Angell M 2004). A greater need is now recognized for channeling R&D resources toward innovative medicines.

The effectiveness of pharmaceutical R&D can be improved through measures such as (i) using evidence from comparative effectiveness research including cost-effectiveness criteria, and (ii) developing personalized medicines, as discussed earlier. Many economists agree that the current patent system is a major reason that large amounts of research occur on drugs with little incremental therapeutic value, in addition to providing inadequate incentives to innovate in novel areas (Hollis, 2004; Stiglitz & Jaidev, 2010; Love & Hubbard, 2007). A panel of experts in the World Health Assembly is considering the merits of lowering prices by delinking R&D costs from pricing, and open collaborative approaches to R&D (Hoetz, Cohen, Mimura, Yamada, &Hoffman, 2013). More effective drugs may lower medical costs through downstream effects, such as decreasing the demand for other medical services and inpatient care and might also lead to a decrease in relapse episodes. The approach to analyze cost-effectiveness of the cancer medicine is already covered under the pricing section.

6. Financial Protection: Public (Drugs) Reimbursement Schemes, Affordable Prepaid Insurance Plans and Income Loss Protection Provisions

A number of new chemotherapies in the market are now being administered orally rather than intravenously and are usually more expensive than intravenous versions that are off patent (IOM, Institute of Medicine, 2014). Another reason for rising cost in recent years is that cancer therapies are becoming targeted with more precise indications, the potential market has become smaller (IOM 2014). The market volume for each cancer drug (that is, the number of patients who can use it), "has halved or decreased by one-third between 2001 and 2013, about the same period of time during which the price of cancer drugs has skyrocketed" (IOM 2014, P 13). Because of their skyrocketing cost, drugs now comprise 35 percent of the cost of cancer care (IOM 2014). Moreover, there has been a dramatic rise in cancer drug prices in recent years due to biologic agents replacing traditional cytotoxic agents. Biologics cost more to develop and produce. Another challenge is that access to cancer drugs is "compounded by drug shortages, which have been increasing for commonly used cancer medications" (Shuman and Emanuel, 2013, cited in IOM 2014).

Escalating cancer drugs and treatment costs warrant an urgent need to protect people against the risks of financial distress and to support all affected families through adequate social security benefits. The following section deals with this issue of financial protection. Empirical studies suggest a strong link between extreme financial distress and worse mortality (Zafar 2016). The above-mentioned link (association) is termed as 'financial toxicity.' Financial toxicity is a grave concern for patients with cancer who are uninsured or under-insured. Zafar explains the relationship between extreme financial distress and greater risk of mortality: 1) poorer subjective well-being, 2) impaired health-related quality of life, and 3) sub-par quality of care. (See figure 1 in Zafar). It has also been found that among survivors, those who faced increased financial burden as a result of cancer care costs have experienced decrease in the quality of life, including increased risk of depressed mood, and a higher frequency of worrying about cancer recurrence and decrease in productivity at work (Fenn et al 2014, Kale & Carroll 2016).

Because cancer care is expensive and requires a long duration of treatment and recovery processes, several issues demand attention. One serious challenge is how to provide access to affordable, quality health care and financial support in case of sickness (International Labour Organization, 2008; Scheil-Adlung, 2014). In addition, in both HICs and LMICs[48], the working poor[49] engaged in part-time, non-standard temporary, and self-employed jobs face a high risk of slipping into the poverty-illness quagmire and the consequent risk of financial impoverishment. Data show that non-standard work accounted for around a third of the total employment in OECD countries in 2013 shared roughly equally between temporary jobs, permanent part-time jobs, and self-employment (Organization for Economic Co-operation and Development, 2015). Among temporary workers, almost half were under age 30 and almost 40% of young workers in the OECD were in non-standard work. Employment precariousness is a social determinant of health (Benach et al., 2014), encompassing both poor employment conditions and a stressful working environment. For developing countries, another thorny and perplexing issue is how to extend income security to the non-pensionable poor and elderly in the informal sector.

Affordability and financial protection against sickness are important dimensions of the ILO's concept of effective access to health care. Cross-national studies, such as those of Lohmann, Frauke, Rostgaard & Spiess (2009), and Brady, Fullerton, and Cross (2010), clearly show that countries with generous welfare programs have lower levels of working poverty than countries with less-generous welfare programs, even when factors like demographics, economic performance, and labor market institutions are taken into account. To address the concerns of old age income security and access to essential health care services for informal economy workers and the elderly poor in LMICs, ILO has suggested a strategy of social protection floors (ILO Recommendation, 2012, No. 202).

In the absence of adequate public or private reimbursement for treatment costs and a considerate social security system, cancer patients may be subjected to grave financial hardships. The causes of cancer-related financial stress and hardships are multifactorial, including medical treatment cost, loss of productivity at work, and other indirect costs. Treatment-related costs can be substantial, including the cost of chemotherapy, radiation and surgery, as well as home healthcare and travel to treatment centers. High insurance premiums, copayments, and income loss raise the risk of cost-related non-adherence (Zafar 2016).

Patients who are employed may experience loss of productivity at work, or total loss of employment and work-related benefits. Household finances may suffer if the patient's family members take time away from work to help with their care. Other less apparent causes of financial burden include child care, domestic help, medical equipment, and special foods and nutritional supplements (Fenn et al., 2014). The average OOP cost for cancer patients over a two-year period in the U.S. is about $4,720 (Davidoff, 2013). The study by Bestvina, Zullig, & Yousuf Zafar (2014) estimates that the average OOP expenses and lost wages for women with breast cancer were $1,455 each month in the United States. Research by the Canadian Cancer Society has reported that nine out of 10 Canadian families touched by the disease run risks of getting pushed to the edge of financial bankruptcy as incomes decline and treatment related costs mount, including child care, traveling expenses, parking costs, unforeseen medical expenses, and gaps in government's safety nets (CCS, 2012). A survey conducted by the Association of Oncology Social Work (AOSW) in 2009 estimated that more than one half (55%) of cancer patients indicated that cancer costs negatively impact their ability to focus on recovery. Among other findings, the survey by AOSW noted that 63% of oncology social workers surveyed said that financial issues reduced patients' compliance with their cancer treatment (Mellace, 2010). It is obvious that cancer treatment-related financial burdens affect patient well-being and recovery.

Financial protection needs to address three major challenges: (i) protecting patients and their families against the risks of financial impoverishment caused by catastrophic OOP expenses, (ii) compensating the patient for the loss of income due to sickness, and (iii) ensuring minimum income security to people in unsecured, temporary, and non-standard work arrangements. Each of these is discussed below.

6.1 Universal Drug Coverage with Public Funding and Affordable Pre-paid Private Health Insurance Plans

Patients undergoing treatment for certain types of cancers can encounter medical costs beyond what their insurance covers. Extensive copayments and/or deductibles, travel costs, loss of income, and home care can cause remarkably high OOP expenditures (Kumthekar et al., 2014).[50] Kumthekar et al reported from the American Cancer Society estimates that 66% of total costs associated with general cancer treatment were non-medical, which could not be covered under basic insurance policies. In the Canadian healthcare setting, "cancer patients do not have access to comprehensive cost coverage once care moves outside of the hospital setting. Hence, patients may be required to pay for such direct medical costs as prescription drugs, complementary and alternative medicine, and home nursing once they are discharged from the hospital" (Longo & Bereza, 2011). The President's Cancer Panel (2018), has endorsed the American Cancer Society Cancer Action Network of limiting the OOP spending to help protect cancer patients from financial toxicity caused by costs of drugs and other components of care.

Two evidence-based approaches are suggested for limiting OOP expenses: (a) universal public coverage programs, and (b) affordable prepaid insurance plans (WHO 2013). These are discussed in the next section.

6.1.1 The Case for Universal Drug Coverage with Public Funding

There has been a growing campaign for universal health coverage at the global level, which includes advocacy for the transformation of healthcare into a universal right, and entails a transition from traditional social insurance as an employment benefit to universal social protection of health—right of citizenship (Knaul et al., 2012). It is generally believed that pharmaceuticals (and health services) should be treated as merit goods, that is, goods consumption should not depend on individual preferences and ability to pay (Docteur & Paris, 2009). Making a strong business case for the universal funding of drugs in Ontario, Canada, Taylor (2014a) showed that "universal funding of oral cancer drugs will save the healthcare system money overall." Emphasizing the economic aspect of universal pharma care, Gagnon (2010) has suggested that the establishment of universal drug coverage (a plan providing first-dollar coverage) policy in Canada could save between 10% and 42%—up to $10.7 billion—of total drug expenditures. While Gagnon concedes that a universal pharma care program would increase prescription drug use an estimated 10% overall, he argues that those additional costs would be more than offset by the cost savings from the adoption of other policies, such as rigorous drug reviews, price negotiations, and nationwide risk pooling, resulting in economies of scale (Morgan, Daw, & Law, 2013).

6.1.2 Mandated Prepaid Health Insurance Protection against Catastrophic Costs

Health insurance—including prescription drug coverage—is a key factor in ensuring that drugs are affordable for cancer patients (The President's Cancer Panel 2018). Many countries do not have a universal coverage policy to protect people against the cost of drugs. To overcome problems associated with individual private insurance markets, Gruber (2010) recommended the "three-legged stool" approach to incremental universalism, which includes insurance market reforms, mandates, and subsidies. The first leg of the stool is aimed to ensure the availability of coverage for those without access to employer-provided or public insurance.[51] Under this coverage, insurers cannot deny or drop coverage based on pre-existing conditions (i.e., guaranteed issue), or vary premiums to reflect health status for limited adjustments such as age and smoking status (i.e., community rating). The second leg required health insurance coverage of adults and mandates that employers provide the coverage. This was proposed to prevent the adverse selection problem (i.e., rising premiums gradually driving healthy individuals out of the non-group market).[52] To assist LMI (Lower middle income) households financially to comply with the mandate, the third leg of the reform allows government subsidies to make insurance affordable for lower income families by way of tax credits that offset the costs. Using the above reform principles, the Patient Protection and Affordable

Care Act of 2010 transformed the non-group insurance market in America.[53] It mandated that most residents have health insurance, significantly expanded public insurance, subsidized private insurance coverage, raised revenues from a variety of new taxes, and reduced and reorganized spending under the nation's largest health insurance plan, Medicare (Gruber, 2011).

Healthcare systems with higher prepaid funds for health care—that is, funds paid by individuals before the event of illness, through social health insurance contributions or taxes—are likely to enhance financial protection by favoring the effective spread of financial risk across all population groups (Moreno-Serra et al., 2011). The extended risk pooling and prepayment are considered as key indicators of progress toward universal coverage across health systems.

In the absence of mandated insurance, millions of families (healthy, young, and affluent) would simply choose to remain uninsured. No country has attained universal population coverage by relying mainly on voluntary contributions to insurance schemes, whether they are run by nongovernmental organizations, commercial companies, communities, or governments. Compulsion, with subsidization for the poor, is a necessary condition for universality (Kutzin, 2012).

Approximately 38% of expenditures on prescription drugs in Canada are financed through private insurance plans (CIHI, 2013[54]), which are voluntary (individual basis) in all provinces except Quebec. In private-employer-provided group insurance, the goal of all insurers is to create large insurance pools with a predictable distribution of medical risk. The non-group (that is, individual and voluntary) insurance market, on the other hand, is not a well-functioning market.

6.2 Protection against Income Loss during Sickness

Disease-related physical impairments prevent people from working or result in a loss of work productivity, reduction in work hours, and ultimately, loss of income to the family. A 2010 Canadian study researched income loss due to cancer on a national basis. It calculated that 91% of households with a cancer diagnosis suffered a loss of income or rise in expenses as a direct result of that diagnosis (Sullivan et al., 2011). The same study revealed that labor participation was reduced by 36%, while income was reduced by 26.5%.[55] These startling numbers provide a context for understanding the ways in which patients, families, and compassionate caregivers are all affected by a cancer diagnosis (Hopkins, Goeree, & Longo, 2010). In many instances, lost income had a larger impact than OOP expenses (Longo, Fitch, Deber, & Williams, 2006). It is estimated that families with a child diagnosed with cancer incurred, on average, more than $28,000 in costs in the first three months following diagnosis (Tsimicalis, 2010). This figure was 40% of an average Canadian family's income in 2011, well above the 4% of income that defines catastrophic drug coverage (Taylor, 2014 a, b). While most countries, including Canada, have disability programs for patients, the eligibility criteria are highly restrictive. Many actually exclude cancer patients, even those with metastatic diseases, from such recourse. The 'Compassionate Care Benefit' provided through Employment Insurance (EI) may provide financial support for a caregiver's eligibility requirements (to get EI benefits for caregivers), but has severe limitations (Canadian Cancer Society, 2012).

A WHO study (2010) found that only one in five individuals worldwide has access to social security protection to help cover lost wages in the event of illness, and that overall, less than half the world's population has any formal social protection. One essential part of social security protection is the provision of paid-sick leave. Paid sick leave aims at improving health outcomes with faster recoveries. It also addresses income security and avoids sickness-induced financial hardship. Paid sick leave is intended to protect the worker's status and income during the period of illness or injury through health and financial protection (Scheil-Adlung & Sandner, 2011). Moreover, it has been found that paid sick leave pays off in terms of health and economic gains for employers, workers, and the economy (Scheil-Adlung & Sandner, 2011).

Table 8 presents the main features of paid sick leave in selected developed countries, ranked high in terms of economic and human development. It provides a comparison by country of employer, or government-provided financial support available to workers facing illness from cancer. Heymann et al. (2009), as shown in this table, have reported that in cases of cancer treatment requiring 50 days of absence, Canada pays employees up to 15 weeks of sick leave at 55% of their salary level. In the case of United States, the evidence presented in Heymann et al. (2009) indicates that it is the only country with no guaranteed paid sick leave. At the other extreme, Luxembourg and Norway provide 100% salary for 50 missed work days. Three more countries also mandate more than 40 days paid sick leave: Finland (47), Austria (45), and Germany

(44); ten countries guarantee between 20 and 40 days of full-time equivalent earnings: Belgium (39), Sweden (38), Denmark (36), the Netherlands (35), Spain (33), Italy (29), Greece (29), Japan (28), France (24), and Canada (22) (Heymann et al., 2009).

Table 8. Main Features of National Paid Sick Day and Paid Sick Leave Systems in Selected High Human Development Index Countries

Country	Min Job Tenure Requirement for 50-day cancer	Sickness pay	Benefit claim
Australia	None	10 days (100% E)	None
Austria	None	6 weeks (100%, E), additional 4 weeks (50%, E) (25%, SI). SI benefits continue for 52 weeks (50%, 60% after 6 weeks)	€3,930 per month
Canada	600 hours work in last 52 weeks or since last claim	12 weeks of job protection (unpaid) 15 weeks (55%, SI)	CAD $42,300 per year
Germany	4 weeks of service	6 weeks (100%, E) If still ill, 78 weeks in a 3-year Period (70%, SI).	Up to 90% of net salary
Luxemburg	None	First 77 days (100%, E [80% reimbursed by SI]) until the end of the month during which the 77th day occurs.	None
Netherlands	None	2 years (70%, E), minimum wage not guaranteed in the 2nd year.	None
UK	None	Up to 28 weeks (£75.40, 20.3%, E). If still ill, 13 weeks of assessment phase and additional periods of main phase (SI).	Flat rate of £75.40 per week for 28 weeks
USA	NA	None	NA

Note. "E" refers to employer sponsored paid sick leave. "SI" refers to social insurance.

Source: Heymann et al., 2009.

Another detailed study by Heymann et al. (2010) compared Canadian policies with data collected on 186 United Nations countries and found that while Canada pays sickness benefits for 15 weeks in case of serious illnesses, globally at least 90 countries provide benefits for at least 26 weeks or until recovery. Moreover, within Canada, only Saskatchewan and Quebec guarantee job protection if sick leave lasts over 12 days. In many places in Europe such as Finland, the UK, Ireland, Iceland, Greece, and Denmark, paid sick leave available to low-wage workers is even more generous than it is for the typical worker (Heymann et al., 2010).

When faced with recurrences of cancer, many survivors experience repeated disruptions in earning power. The Canadian Cancer Action Network in Manitoba (Canadian Cancer Society, 2012) reports that if the cancer returns, or a second round of treatment is required, the person will not qualify for sick benefits unless the person has worked a minimum of 600 hours (approximately 16 weeks, or four months for a typical full-time job) since their last claim. Another serious problem is the lack of any Canadian laws to protect those people with chronic diseases or those who need to take time off when diagnosed with cancer. Survivors face additional challenges to find health insurance, as they are considered high-risk candidates due to the potential for recurrence of the cancer (Soliman & Agresta, 2008).

Recognizing the need for paid sick leave, governments in most countries have included guaranteed paid sick leave in legislation—whether state-funded, in the form of social and national insurances, or employer-based schemes (Scheil-Adlung & Sandner, 2011).

Paid sick leave is also frequently regulated in collective (bargaining or labor) agreements. Better financial support (and income stability) in times of serious illness, at a level adequate to support cancer patients' needs during such a stressful and exceptional life event, would significantly offset the increased costs for patients and caregivers, making cancer expenses less of a burden and reducing the anxiety of individuals and families during a very difficult time (Canadian Cancer Society, 2012).

The ILO has proposed a social health protection plan as a cushion against the economic burdens of poor health. Social health protection is defined by the ILO as a series of public or publicly organized and mandated private measures against social distress and economic loss, caused by the reduction of productivity, stoppage or reduction of earnings, or the cost of necessary treatment that can result from ill health. Social protection needs to be distinguished from traditional employment-based social security because it is not dependent on labor market participation. In countries where a large segment of the population is non-salaried[56]—including independent workers and non-participants in the labor market—universal social protection is more relevant because it goes beyond securing employment benefits. The ultimate purpose of social protection is to expand human capabilities, which allows citizens to fully enjoy their economic, social, and cultural rights, regardless of their employment status (Knaul et al., 2012).

6.3 Income Security to Working Poor in High Income Countries

According to the OECD, poverty has increased over the past decade in a number of OECD countries, and on average in the mid-2000s slightly more than one person in ten lived in a household with disposable income below 50% of the median income (OECD, 2009). The growing incidence of temporary and involuntary part-time work and the persistence of informal jobs—which are significantly less well remunerated than permanent, full-time work—partly explains falling labor shares, rising in-work poverty[57], and income inequalities in some of the advanced countries (ILO, OECD, 2015). Evidence of employment trends from OECD countries does not support the contention that temporary work is a stepping-stone toward permanent employment. Instead, younger workers in many countries, especially those with temporary work contracts, have experienced a lower chance of moving on to more stable jobs. For Canada, the evidence suggests that once engaged in non-standard employment, the majority of workers remain in such jobs for an extended period of time (Kapsalis & Tourigny, 2004). Many such workers have no health insurance or pay for it out of pocket. These working poor have barely enough regular income flow to meet their basic living expenses and family responsibilities, let alone cover additional health premiums.

The spread of in-work poverty has raised concerns at the international level and warranted the need to design anti-poverty measures to shield labor rights and to extend social security to workers in less secure forms of employment. Some suggested anti-poverty proposals include: (i) introducing well targeted and generous in-work benefits with strong distributional consequences for individuals facing particular labor market challenges, combined with a binding minimum wage set (OECD, 2009; Dabla-Norris et al., 2015); (ii) increasing public spending on well-designed active labor market policies aimed at supporting job search and skill matching (OECD, 2009); (iii) executing policies that reduce labor market dualism, such as gaps in employment protection between permanent and temporary workers; and (iv) implementing pro-equity policies in countries experiencing growing income inequality gaps, as reflected in the increasing proportions of working households with an income below 60% of median income (Dabla-Norris et al., IMF, 2015; OECD, 2015).

7. Low and Middle-Income Countries: Pricing of Cancer Drugs and Social Security Protection Issues

In economically poor nations, where a large section of the population lives below the poverty line, the high cost of cancer drugs is a matter of great concern. The poorest countries face the highest prices, relative to their mean per capita income (Danzon, Towse, & Mulcahy, 2011). In South Asia, for example, the probability of incurring catastrophic health expenditure from hospitalization is estimated to be 1.6 times higher for cancer than for a communicable disease such as pneumonia (Knaul et al., 2015). People in the lower rungs of the social and economic hierarchy in these countries are most vulnerable to the illness-poverty trap as they are more exposed to nutritional, environmental, and lifestyle-related risk factors.

The high cost of cancer drugs is severely limiting the access to treatment in economically poor nations. In addition, a large share of rural populations living far away from public health centers or hospitals bear an additional burden of transportation and other indirect costs. Concerns have been expressed at the international level (World Trade Organization ministerial conference in DOHA[58] 2001) about the adverse effects of patent protection on the access to patented medicines in low-income countries (LIMCs).

Limited government budgets for healthcare and undeveloped prepaid health insurance schemes are major contributors to the heavy reliance on OOP payments for medical expenses. This results in the adverse consequence of inequitable access to tertiary health care for people with poor socioeconomic status (Patel et al., 2015). As discussed previously, informal economy workers and the poor do not have social protection in terms of old age income security and access to essential health care services. Though access to social security is internationally acknowledged as a human right, informal workers are generally excluded from health and income protection policies that are available to workers in the formal sector. This population makes up a large proportion in developing countries, with the percentage of the workforce in the informal sector ranging from 7%—84%. Finding fiscal space to finance basic social protection has become a necessity for these countries.

The issues mentioned above, ranging from high drug prices relative to the per capita level in developing countries, low priority of health sector in the public budget, predominance of the informal sector and people below poverty line, and the near absence of social security beyond the formal sector, are reviewed in the following subsections.

7.1 Pricing of Drugs and Affordability[59] Issues

Current systems of pricing of pharmaceutical drugs and incentive mechanisms for stimulating R&D have come under scrutiny due to their limitations in delivering affordable medicines to people in economically poor nations. Evidence shows that the prices of cancer medicines seem commensurate neither with demand, nor with a country's purchasing power (WHO 2018). Several studies have acknowledged the need to address the market failures associated with the current patent-based pricing and intellectual property rights system from the perspective of low-income countries. To meet the affordability and access challenges in LMICs, reports and research studies have examined several proposals, including, (a) 'differential pricing' (Danzon, Towse, & Mulcahy, 2011, 2003, 2013) and compulsory licensing systems (DOHA, 2001; Danzon, 2003; Danzon, 2013); (b) devoting more resources to health care services (i.e., fiscal space for health care) by governments in poor countries, as well as, (c) adopting measures to minimize private OOP expenses.

Each of these is briefly considered below.

7.1.1 Differential Pricing

"The finding of higher prices, relative to per capita income, in lower income countries, appears to be inconsistent with optimal differential pricing framework" (Danzon, 2013). It is now widely acknowledged that differential pricing, (also known as tiered pricing), can play an important role in ensuring access to existing essential drugs at affordable prices, especially in low-income countries, while allowing the patent system to continue to play its role of providing incentives for R&D into new drugs (Danzon, 2003; WHO, 2001). Differential pricing is sensitive to health systems' ability to pay (WHO 2018). "Differential pricing is based on the price discrimination and Ramsey pricing theories, which give the criteria for an efficient structure of relative prices" (Danzon, 2013). The economic concept of price discrimination is applicable in situations where consumers are segmented into different groups, or tiers, and pharmaceutical companies are able to charge lower prices in highly price-sensitive markets such as poorer countries, than in less price-sensitive markets such as richer countries. In lower income countries, low per capita income and the absence of universal insurance coverage results in highly price-sensitive markets. The Ramsey optimal pricing solution implies that prices should differ across market segments in inverse relation to their demand elasticities (Danzon, 2003). Differential pricing is called 'equity pricing' when the intention is to improve the affordability of medicine in low income settings (Management Sciences for Health, 2012; Danzon, 2003).

Differential pricing is feasible where there are substantial fixed costs and the variable, or marginal, costs of production are relatively low. In the pharmaceutical industry, R&D is a global joint cost that benefits consumers in high-income, middle-income, and low-income countries, worldwide. Economists such as Danzon (2003) and others have explained how differential pricing can be in the interests of both consumers in poor countries and manufacturers, provided there is no diversion of low-priced products into high-income markets (parallel trade) and no external referencing.[60] The WHO (2001) also agreed "that differential pricing of essential drugs is fully compatible with the TRIPS Agreement[61] and should not require countries to forgo any flexibility they have under it." Opportunities for parallel trade and external reference pricing can be avoided if payers in developing countries and pharmaceutical companies negotiate contracts that include confidential rebates (Danzon, 2003).

In recent years, another variant of differential pricing, "Value-based" differential pricing (VBDP), is used to achieve appropriate prices based on an incremental cost-effectiveness ratio threshold set by payers in each country (Danzon, 2013, 2011; Lopert, Lang, Hill, & Henry, 2002). Danzon (2011) recommends that "countries and payers set their own cost-effectiveness thresholds to reflect how much they are willing to pay for 'health gain'—in other words, for a measured improvement in the health of a person or a population." Additionally, these authors remark that VBDP offers a practical approach to determine absolute prices, as well as relative prices. In economically poor countries without a universal coverage system, the demand of patients' OOP expenses may reflect their willingness to pay for expected incremental QALY benefits, given good information on product quality and effectiveness (Danzon, 2013).

7.1.2 Compulsory Licensing

Compulsory licensing policy is another policy option to control prices of drugs in low income countries. Compulsory licensing is the practice by which a government allows a third party to produce or sell the patented product or process without the patentee's consent. It is one of the flexibilities in patent protection included in the World Trade Organization's (WTO) agreement on intellectual property. The TRIPS Agreement, Section 93 of the International Protection (IP) Code, allows a license to exploit a patented invention even without the agreement of the patent owner under circumstances of extreme urgency, such as national emergencies. The DOHA Declaration recognized the inability of poor countries to pay for essential medications for its citizens.

A current issue of debate is the DOHA Declaration provision that allows members to use compulsory licenses in circumstances of a public health emergency. Western drug makers have often accused India and other developing countries of using public health as a pretext to boost the generic pharmaceutical industries. International debate was sparked recently in India when Bayer lost its bid to block a cheap version of the cancer drug Nexavar from the Indian market. India subsequently issued a compulsory license that allowed Natco Pharma, the manufacturer, to sell Nexavar for just $173 a month, compared with the $5,500 a month charged by the German company.

Danzon (2003) compares the economic case for using differential pricing with the option of using compulsory licensing and suggests that the "option of compulsory licensing of patented products to generic manufacturers may be important if they truly have lower production costs, or originators charge prices above marginal cost, despite market separation."

7.2 Creating Additional Fiscal Space for the Financial and Social Protection of the Poor

Most LMICs are falling short of health financing benchmarks set out by international organizations on the basis of the comparative development experience of HICs. Many countries in Africa and Asia are facing large legal coverage deficits. For example, in India more than 80% of the population is not legally covered (ILO, 2014). The deficit in legal health coverage in developing countries is compounded by access deficit indicators, namely the deficits in the number of health workers needed to deliver services, per capita health spending, and OOP expenses. One of the factors contributing to deficits in effective access is the high share of OOP expenses as a source of health financing in these countries (see Table 9). The ILO (2008) estimates that people in low-income and LMICs, such as Cambodia, India, and Pakistan, have to cover more than 50% of their own health expenditures, whereas people in upper middle and high-income countries shoulder under 30% of their healthcare financial burden.

Table 9. Sources of National Health Spending for Regions and Selected Countries 2013

Regions/ Countries	THE per GDP (%)	Domestic GHE per THE (%)	Prepaid per THE (%)	OOP per THE (%)
Global	6.0	56.5	12.0	20.0
High income	6.4	56.9	30.4	12.6
Upper-middle income	5.4	56.4	16.5	27.0
Lower-middle income	4.7	36.6	13.2	49.0
Low income	4.6	31.2	7.4	49.7
Canada	10.9	67.0	20.1	12.9
France	11.7	73.4	20.4	6.2

Regions/ Countries	THE per GDP (%)	Domestic GHE per THE (%)	Prepaid per THE (%)	OOP per THE (%)
Germany	11.3	74.5	14.6	10.9
Netherlands	12.0	83.8	11.7	5.0
USA	17.1	42.0	48.7	9.3
UK	9.1	81.8	10.2	8.0
Bangladesh	3.7	33.1	6.2	57.7
China	5.6	56.2	15.8	28.0
India	3.9	33.0	15.7	50.9
Pakistan	2.6	33.5	11.5	52.2
Thailand	4.5	78.5	12.2	9.3
Jordan	7.2	63.3	14.5	20.2

Note. 'THE' refers to total health expenditure, GDP refers to gross domestic product, GHE refers to government health expenditure, and OOP refers to OOP expenses. Material sourced from: Dieleman, J. L., Templin, T., Sadat, N., Reidy, P., Chapin, A., Foreman, K. Kurowski, C. (2016). National spending on health by source for 184 countries between 2013 and 2040. The Lancet. 387(10037), 2521–2535.

Using Thailand as benchmark, ILO (2008), Table 10 presents estimates for China and India on selected social indicators of health protection. China and India, two of the most populated countries of the world, together account for 36.41% of total world population and are facing huge economic and human costs from disease. Both of these growing economies have aging populations, increasingly westernized lifestyles, relatively disenfranchised subpopulations, serious contamination of the environment, and uncontrolled cancer-causing communicable infections (Goss et al., 2014).

Table 10. Selected Indicators of Social Health Protection in China, India and Thailand (data for latest year available)

Selected Indicators	China	India	Thailand
Total formal coverage as % of population	23.9	5.7	97.7
Staff related national access deficit as% of population	34	56.0	Benchmark country for estimating access deficit (source (a), P26)
Public social protection expenditure for persons of active age-sickness, maternity, employment injury, and disability (% of GDP)	1.55	0.10	0.20
Estimates of legal coverage for old age as a % of the working-age population-(non-contributory)	6.8	-	38.2

Note. (a) International Labour Organization, (2008). Social health protection. An ILO strategy towards universal access to health care, In Social security policy briefings. Geneva, Switzerland: International Labour Organization. International Labour Organization, (2014): World Social Protection Report 2014/2015, Building economic recovery, inclusive development and social justice.

These high percentage OOP expenses translate to catastrophic expenditures in the case of long-term and expensive illnesses like cancer. Empirical evidence from country studies indicates that a 1% increase in the proportion of total health expenditure provided by OOP payments is associated with an average increase in the proportion of households facing catastrophic payments of 2.2% (McIntyre & Meheus, 2014). In many LMICs that rely extensively on direct OOP payments to fund health services, poor households are more likely to suffer disproportionately from the financial effects resulting from this lack of social protection. According to Kankeu, Saksena, Xu, & Evans (2013), "To meet the costs, households reported taking unsecured loans, using savings, or selling household assets, all of which can lead to longer-term problems for the household." The low level of public expenditure on health as a ratio of gross domestic product (GDP) in developing nations is another reason for large deficits in effective access. The Chatham house report (McIntyre, 2014) mentions that those LMICs that currently have relatively low levels of government expenditure are able to create budgetary room(fiscal space) to allow them to devote an increasing amount of resources to provide essential health care services and provide basic income security to all of its people. Finding fiscal space for critical economic and social investments is necessary for achieving the goals of sustained human development of children and women, and for realizing human rights (ILO 2017).[62] Evidence indicates that when government health spending was greater than 5% of GDP, few households faced financial difficulties related to health costs (Dieleman et al., 2016). Table 6 shows that for some Asian developing countries, including India, Pakistan, and Bangladesh, this ratio is below the average found in low-income countries, which indicates a severe affordability of care problem.

Creating fiscal space to extend basic income security to those not covered by the formal sector is a warranted action from an equity and human rights perspective. In the absence of social security provisions beyond the formal sector, persons who are too ill or too old to work in their informal occupations may suffer severe financial hardships. According to the WHO (2010), in "typically low-income countries, more than 50% of the working-age population works in the informal sector without access to income replacement." In India, 67.5% of those employed were found to be working in the informal sector in 2012 (de Arruda, 2015). Workers and their families in the informal economy remain uncovered, unless fiscal space is created in the national budget to address their health care and basic income needs. One promising way to extend social security in the area of income security is through non-contributory, tax-financed cash transfers. As an indicator of the non-contributory source, Table 11 presents estimates of legal coverage for old age as a percentage of the working-age population. China and India lag behind Thailand's performance in this respect. Though there are doubts that a universal non-contributory pension system could be affordable in poor countries, the estimates suggest that through the allocation of less than 3% of GDP, a country may be able to support their universal non-contributory pension systems (Johnson & Williamson, 2008).

To expand access to healthcare for all and income security, ILO has suggested national floors of social protection (ILO Recommendation No. 222). The recommendation makes explicit reference to people in the informal economy. Only a few developing countries have adopted a universal scheme for all residents that guarantees access to health care protection programs and a flat pension rate for all residents above a determined age. The next section compares India and China with respect to their initiatives regarding social protection floors.

7.3 Elements of Social Protection Floor: China and India

To meet the challenges of providing adequate financial protection against the risks of catastrophic OOP expenses, both countries have introduced innovative financing programs of cancer treatment for uninsured and poor people. The predominance of the rural and informal sector workforce has required policies to extend income security to people outside the formal sector. Table 11 presents a summary and comparative view of policies in these countries.

Table 11. Social Protection Plans for the Uninsured: India and China

Access to health care services.	Pension plans covering non-working poor, old, and people in the informal sector.
India	India
RSBY and state-run insurance programs: Targets people below the poverty line (means-tested). The Vajpayee Arogyashree Scheme, Karnataka: Targets people below the poverty line. Rajiv Aarogyasri Scheme, Andhra Pradesh: Targets people below the poverty line.	NOAPS: Targets people above 65 years, under the poverty line or with no regular means of subsistence (means-tested).

China	China
NCMS: Targets the rural population, elderly, children, non-working poor. Medical Assistance Scheme: Targets rural population with financial assistance as well as exemptions for catastrophic health expenditures to poor and low income. URBMI: A voluntary scheme covering children, students, elderly, disabled, and non-working poor.	NRSPS: Targets rural residents 16 years of age and older (students not included) who are not enrolled in basic pension insurance.

Source: National Old Age Pension Scheme

Note. RSBY refers to Rashtriya Swasthya Bima Yojana, NOAPS refers to the National Old Age Pension Scheme, NCMS refers to New Medical Cooperative Medical Scheme, URBMI refers to the Urban Residence Basic Medical Insurance Scheme, and NRSPS refers to New Rural Social Pension Scheme. Material sourced from: ILO (2011): Sharing Innovative Experiences, Successful Social Protection Floor Experiences volume 18, UNDP 2011; Help Age International (2013): Pension Watch-Briefing on social protection in the old age, pension coverage in China www.pension-watch.net.

The following subsection outlines the elements of social protection floors in these countries. The focus is mainly on the healthcare and income security coverage for the economically-socially poor, old, and informal sector employees.

7.3.1 Social Protection Policy Initiatives in India

Contributory, but heavily subsidized, government-supported health insurance programs for the formal sector currently cover roughly 5% of India's population. To provide health insurance protection to poor and informal communities, the central government developed the "National Rural Health Mission" (NRHM) and the "Rashtriya Swasthya Bima Yojana" (RSBY). According to the Public Health Foundation of India (2011), the "NRHM attempts to ensure universal coverage through the tax-based route while the RSBY is expected to provide financial risk protection to the underprivileged, informal households, through insurance mechanisms." Currently RSBY covers only the population below the poverty line, using the Below Poverty Line number derived from the Planning Commission. Sood et al. (2014) states, "To meet the need for tertiary care, while providing financial security to people with low incomes, several states in India have rolled out social insurance programs that provide free tertiary care for a targeted range of services, including oncology, to households below the poverty line." As mentioned above, these insurance programs are financed by taxes and typically do not require premiums or user fees from beneficiaries. It is estimated that the percentage of population covered by the insurance schemes has accelerated from about 75 million people covered (roughly 16 million family beneficiaries) in 2007 to an estimated 302 million people in 2010, about one-fourth of the population (Public Health Foundation of India, 2011).

India's performance in regard to implementing social health protection is poor when compared with other countries at a similar level of development. Despite a higher income per capita and two decades of sustained economic growth, public health expenditure as a proportion of GDP remains low at just 1.28% of the country's GDP in 2013–14 (Patel, 2015). A consequence of the relatively small public expenditure for health care is the high OOP expenditure incurred for health care (Patel, 2015). While many insurance schemes have proliferated in the past years (Patel, 2015), these have a limited effect on financial risk protection due to relatively low coverage limits and exclusions for drugs, outpatient visits, and investigations, which account for a large part of health care expenditure. Households pay a higher share of health expenditures on outpatient care, especially drugs. Most schemes limit expenses through annual family caps. Future success will require determined and committed action by the government, taking into consideration the rapid epidemiologic transition in India to more non-communicable, or chronic diseases.

The social pension in India is means-tested but only reaches approximately 12% of older people. Strong cases have been made to introduce a universal pension scheme to cover the non-working poor and working population in the unorganized/informal sector (Sanyal & Singh, 2013). India has the lowest absolute level of social security coverage, both in terms of access to health care and old age social security pensions, among the BRICS countries[63] (de Arruda, 2015). India's social protection policies are fragmented sub-national initiatives.

India needs to take lessons from other developing countries (i.e., Thailand and China), and recognize the interconnectedness of social security and economic policy and, in particular, ensure a minimum floor of protection in old age.

7.3.2 Social Protection Policy Initiatives in China

In China, health coverage is offered through three public insurance programs examined in Table 8. The New Rural Cooperative Medical Scheme (NRCMS) launched in 2003 to cover the rural population; the Urban Resident Basic Medical Insurance (URBMI) launched in 2007 to target the unemployed, children, students, and the disabled in urban areas; and the Urban Employee Basic Medical Insurance (UEBMI) launched in 1998 to offer employment-based insurance program. The Medical Financial Assistance program, which is financed by central and local governments, covers premiums for the New Cooperative Medical Scheme (NCMS) and URBMI, medical expenses beyond insurance limits, and temporary financial support for medical expenses for the poor (Yerramilli & Jiang, 2013). China, with heavy support from government subsidies that account for 75% and 85% of the premiums of NRCMS and URBMI respectively, achieved universal coverage in 2011 (Yu, 2015). Both NRCMS and URBMI, which initially covered only inpatient services, were broadened to cover outpatient services in 2010 (Yu, 2015). At the national level, the proportion of OOP expenditures to total national health expenditures has significantly decreased from 60% in 2001 to 35% in 2011 (Yu, 2015). UEBMI provides a more comprehensive service package and more financial protection than NRCMS and URBMI (Meng, Fang, Liu, Yuan, & Xu, 2015), since the insurance premiums collected under UEBMI are much higher than the other two plans.

Under the New Rural Social Pension Scheme (NRSPS), rural residents aged 60 and over are eligible to receive a monthly basic pension of 55 yuan, paid for by the government (Quan, 2013). Two major factors explain the rapid expansion of the NRSPS, including the growing financial strength and political will of the Chinese government. The Chinese experience demonstrates that the universality of pension can be achieved by combining contributory schemes and non-contributory social pensions, in line with the Social Protection Floors Recommendation (ILO No. 202, ILO, 2015). By the end of 2013, about 80% of the population of working-age and older citizens, regardless of their employment and contribution histories, were covered under the pension system (ILO, 2015).

Despite this impressive success, several challenges remain. According to Quan (2013), "Coverage of the working-age population is still far from universal pension benefits and sustainability in the face of a rapidly aging population remains a concern." Benefit levels (measured as a percentage of PPP $1.25 per day) of pension under NRSPS in China is above that of India, though quite low compared to others BRICS countries (Quan, 2013).

8. Prevention of Cancer

Cancer is a major public health issue, ranked as a leading cause of morbidity and mortality worldwide. In view of the complexity of cancer and the scale of its consequences, governments are implementing a spectrum of interventions to mitigate the current and future impacts of cancer (WHO 2018). Interventions need to aim at eliminating or minimizing population exposure to cancer-related risk factors. The need for such preventive policies is critical in all countries, more particularly those undergoing economic transition. This global increase in the cancer burden and its disproportionate impact on economically developing countries can be attributed to three important factors (Thun et al 2009): (i) growth and aging of populations; (b) the entrenchment of modifiable risk factors (particularly cigarette smoking, Western diet and physical inactivity) in developing countries and (c) the slower decline in cancers related to infectious etiologies in low-income countries than in high-income countries. Economically poor countries are currently ill equipped to provide necessary patient care and face an imminent disproportionate impact of the projected increase in the future cancer burden (Bray et al 2015). Estimates show that approximately 70% of deaths from cancer occur in LMICs (WHO 2018 Cancer Factsheet #297). There is also a medical consensus that a substantial proportion of the worldwide burden of cancer can be prevented through the application of existing cancer control knowledge, including tobacco control, vaccination (for liver and cervical cancers), early detection, and the promotion of physical activity and healthy dietary patterns (Torre et al

2015).

One suggested route to design an effective strategy is to lower the incidence of cancer through prevention. Prevention strategies are policy interventions that aim to reduce the incidence[64] and recurrence of cancer disorders. According to a WHO report (2002, P vii),[65] "Improved cancer control will, to a substantial degree, relate to prevention strategies and early detection programme, including information campaigns and population-based screening programme." This approach offers the greatest public health potential and the most cost-effective long-term method of cancer control (WHO 2002). There are three categories of prevention policies: primary, secondary, and tertiary. Primary prevention aims to reduce the incidence of disease (White et al 2013), and it starts from identifying the causes of cancer and limiting or removing the exposure. Secondary prevention of cancer, or screening, involves the use of examinations and tests to detect a cancer as early as possible, before signs and symptoms would cause a patient to seek care (Eddy 1986). According to Eddy, the value of early detection lies in the possibility of detecting the cancer when it is still localized and more easily curable. Tertiary prevention refers to interventions designed to arrest the progress of an established disease and to control its negative consequences. Tertiary prevention, thus, refers to care aimed at reducing morbidity and disability in people diagnosed with and being treated for disease (Jacobsen & Andrykowski 2015).

8.1 Primary Prevention Policies

Primary prevention is considered to be particularly effective way to fight cancer since between one third and one half of cancers are preventable based on present knowledge of risk factors (Vineis and Wild2014). Primary prevention policies include: (a) controlling the use of tobacco, (b) improving dietary habits and physical activity among people, (c) increasing the availability of vaccines against hepatitis B virus (HBV) and human papilloma virus (HPV) in countries where they are most needed(Thun et al 2009), and (d) reducing exposure to physical environmental risks.

(a) Tobacco and Alcohol Use Control Programs: Reduction in tobacco use provides the largest single opportunity to prevent nearly one third of cancer deaths through the application of existing knowledge (Jemal et al 2008). Increasing tobacco excise taxes and enacting smoke-free laws have been found to be an increasingly effective approach. The WHO Oral Health Programme provides useful guidelines for controlling and global surveillance systems for preventing risks factors of oral cancer. Additionally, effective prevention policies also need to recognize that adolescent period is a very sensitive phase of life when children in schools get exposed to peer and group influence. Medical science attests that adolescence as the key period of development of substance use disorders with striking increases in substance use disorders across adolescents into early adulthood.

To control the onset of the use of psychoactive substances during the adolescent phase, good parenting skills, and school-based resilience building programs can play very effective role. Active parent involvement includes parents spending more time in communicating with their children. Authoritative and responsive parenting as well as school based educational programs on developing skills in social competence and self-regulation and peer resistance training are considered to be effective in reducing or preventing substance use in early stages (Cohen, Richardson, LaBree 1994; Urberg et al 1997; Petrie, Bunn & Byrne 2006). Parenting style is considered to exert an important influence on children's indulgence in alcohol and tobacco use as well as in academic achievement. Cohen and Rice (1997) have provided evidence that parenting styles and adolescents' perceptions of them were associated with child achievement and substance use. Authoritative parenting style, in contrast to authoritarian[66] or permissive parenting, has been shown to assist young children and adolescents develop instrumental competence which is characterized by psychosocial maturity, cooperation with peers and adults, responsible independence, and academic success.

(b) Improving Dietary Intake through All Stages of Life: Effective environmental strategies are required to promote the intake of healthy diet. It is suggested that grocery stores, superstores, farmers' markets and community settings (like Churches) where groups of people interact offer important potential for improving eating patterns (Glanz & Yaroch (2004). Glanz & Yaroch suggest that initiatives like expanding offerings of prepared foods, precut and clean vegetables, and take-out foods in grocery and superstores are promising examples of promoting the increased fruit and vegetable intake. Promotion and pricing factors supported by public health agencies can help to increase the consumption of nutritious food. Changing parental eating habits through providing educational materials for parent–child use at home, including public health campaigns combining social and news media for limiting intake of high-fat and low-nutrient dense foods can serve as parent-focused behavioral intervention on parent and child eating changes (Epstein et al 2001)

(c) Early Life Exposures Strategy and the Significance of Maternal Dietary and Nutritional Programs: The prevention of cancer should start before conception; before becoming pregnant, mothers should ideally maintain a healthy weight and avoid excessive weight gain during pregnancy (Uauy and Solomons 2005, P2934S). As suggested by these authors, key micronutrients are important for normal embryonic development and fetal growth. Findings suggest that in utero exposures may indirectly influence cancer risk by modifying biological pathways associated with carcinogenesis (Clark and Joshu 2017).

Reducing the emergence of problems during early stages of development should have a substantial effect on reducing the burden in later years. Simmen & Simmen (2011) focusing on three major cancers namely breast, colorectal, and liver, suggest anti-obesity strategies for children to decrease their long-term cancer risk. Efforts to increase the intake of vegetables and fruits, beginning from early years of children's growth stages, can play an important role in cancer prevention. It is suggested that in addition to the role of parents in fostering nutritional dietary habits among children, childcare centers represent an important dietary environment for reaching both parents and children (Lunch Is In The Bag, Sweitzer et al 2010). In the United States, the National Cancer Institute launched a national media campaign in 1991 that leveraged supermarket displays, community interventions through schools, dieticians, worksites, and churches to disseminate knowledge about the benefits of improved dietary habits (Steinmetz and Porter 1996).

(d) Increasing the Availability of Vaccines and Preventing Chronic Infections: As pointed out previously in section 2, infections from certain viruses, bacteria, and parasites have been identified as strong risk factors for specific cancers. Attempts to control chronic infections caused by viruses, bacteria and parasites can help developing countries, particularly, to reduce the risk of cancer substantially. These chronic infections contribute to about one third of the world's cancer burden (Ames et al 1993). Vaccines against HPV may help protect against some of the cancers, such as cervical, anal, and throat. Getting the Hepatitis B vaccine to help prevent HBV infection may therefore lower some people's risk of getting liver cancer (American Cancer Society, Cancer Vaccines).[67]

(e) Limiting Exposures to Environmental Pollution: Environmentally related diseases arising from industrial pollutants and exposures to carcinogens through air, water, and food are preventable. For limiting exposures to environmental pollutants, Perera (1993) recommends policy measures that combine the strategy of controlling pollutants after they have been produced ("mopping up") with the policy interventions aiming at preventing their generation ("turning off the faucet"). Control measures to reduce air pollution from traffic have been found successful in decreasing exposure to diesel exhaust gases, and thus may contribute to the prevention of lung cancer (WHO 2011). "Banning the use of asbestos will prevent linked lung cancer and mesothelioma and will also prevent asbestosis, a non-malignant fibrotic condition of the lungs" (WHO 2011). Efforts towards building online information and databases that list chemicals and their toxicity, developing safer alternatives to chemicals, stimulating a new stream of materials research, development, and production, as well as designing toxicological testing of harmful chemicals (Kriebel, Hoppin, Jacobs 2016; Perera 1993) are few examples of preventive interventions. As a preventive strategy against the exposure of UV rays, the study by Narayanan et al (2011) suggests the following protective measures: (i) minimizing sun exposure (seeking shade) during peak hours, (2) wearing sun-protective clothing (including hats with a brim all around, wrap-around sunglasses, which block both UVA and UVB rays, etc.), (3) using sunscreen with both UVA/UVB & physical blocks on your body and lips, and (4) avoiding tanning beds/lamps.

To control environment-related progression of cancer burden, WHO (2011) recommends countries to encourage research on genetic and epigenetic interactions with environmental risk factors in order to support the development of evidence-based preventive strategies.

As mentioned previously, a primary prevention strategy is the practice of avoiding the causes of a disease in order to prevent getting it in the first place. Summarily speaking, a substantial proportion of the worldwide burden of cancer could be prevented through the application of existing cancer control knowledge and by implementing these types of programs for tobacco control, vaccination (for liver and cervical cancers), and early detection (regular mammography), as well as public health campaigns promoting physical activity and healthier dietary intake (Jemal et al 2011, Prochaska et al 2013).

Of the predicted 20 million new cancer cases by 2025, the greatest increases are anticipated in low-income countries and longer-term planning is needed to reduce the future cancer burden through resource-appropriate interventions (Ferlay et al 2015). Ferlay and colleagues draw attention to the poor surveillance system in LMICs since in many LMICs the population-based cancer registries are not available. Timely and accurate cancer statistics are crucial to identify priorities for cancer control strategies at the national level. The Global Initiative for Cancer Registry Development (GICR),[68] a global partnership launched in 2011, is working to increase the coverage and quality of registries in LMICs, which will aid countries in the prioritization and evaluation of national cancer control plans.

9. Summary and Discussion

Despite considerable progress in our understanding of cancer disease and the ability of HICs to reduce cancer death rates, a persistently growing incidence of cancer has, however, become a serious challenge of public health policy in nearly all countries Cancer is now the third leading cause of death as of 2007 evidence (Thun et al 2007). Due to the continuing global demographic and epidemiologic transitions, the incidence rate of cancer is projected to increase over the next decades, particularly in LMICs. Another disconcerting challenge for payers, patients, caregivers, and oncologists is the rapid escalating cost of modern anticancer medication.

Rapidly escalating cancer drug prices have raised disquieting concerns about the affordability and accessibility of life-saving drugs and treatment. Affordability, availability, and timely access to effective new medications are some of the major issues facing cancer patients in countries at all income levels. At present, cancer patients and caregivers are subjected to severe financial distress and impoverishment in most countries due to high OOP expenses and insufficient protection provisions against the loss of income, resulting from severe physical impairments and psychological stress. Another ominous development is the increase, over the past two decades, in the number of working poor living below the median income level in middle- and high-income nations. The economically downtrodden and socially disadvantaged either do not seek treatment or face increasing risk of financial bankruptcy. In reality, prices of drugs tend to be higher than by any conception of value in terms of clinical or wider benefits for patients (OECD Health at Glance 2015 Ch 2).

Restraining the escalating cancer drug prices calls for addressing the issue of declining R&D productivity trends and reforming the drugs pricing system. Regarding the productivity conundrum, the present study has analyzed both the efficiency and effectiveness aspects of the drug discovery and development process. Improving efficiency requires the adoption of strategic measures that modernize the drug development process, including the introduction of novel clinical trial designs. The most popular strategic initiatives include open models of research partnerships between academia and pharmaceutical companies, stronger reliance on pre-competitive research at the early stages of drug discovery, and the use of novel adaptive design of clinical trials. Increasing public investment in biomedical research is necessary so that frontier technologies are in the public domain at the outset. Regulatory approval procedures need to facilitate faster approval of drugs without compromising the safety standards.

In order to improve R&D effectiveness, most countries are attempting to link the prices of new medicines to their therapeutic value, instead of their financial value. The application of the value-based pricing approach is expected to incentivize the development of more cost-effective drugs. Cost-effectiveness and comparative effectiveness methodologies provide one mechanism to better align the use of available resources to optimize health benefits (Smith & Hillner, 2011).

Another factor contributing to escalating costs is the present system of pharmaceutical patent and market exclusivity (intellectual property rights) environment. Evidence indicates that under the prevailing patent system, "research spending gets misdirected into products which add little therapeutic value to the medicine chest" (Hollis, 2008). One potential solution to mitigate this issue is the replacement of granted monopolies with cash prizes for successful development of new and innovative drugs (Hollis, 2008; Love & Hubbard, 2007; Stiglitz & Jayadev, 2010). Under prize fund schemes, rewards for innovation are geared to support the proven therapeutic value of a drug (Love & Hubbard, 2007). Linking rewards directly to the improvements in health outcomes has the added benefit of driving investment toward treatments that address unmet needs.

Along with the need for restraining costs and prices of drugs, there is a pressing requirement of safeguarding families against the imminent danger of financial turbulence in case of a cancer diagnosis. The public health care system and access to publicly-funded drugs play vital roles in shielding cancer patients and caregivers against financial insolvency caused by catastrophic OOP expenses and income loss from work. Private insurance plans for drug coverage, unless properly regulated, are unaffordable for many, and exclude people with pre-existing conditions. The absence of prepaid "mandatory" health insurance plans, particularly in low-income countries, leave many at risk of financial catastrophe and impoverishment if they are diagnosed with cancer. Inadequate provision of paid sick leave as compensation for the loss of income can seriously endanger the patient's ability to continue the treatment, and hence, the recovery process. In addition, a substantial section of the world population is comprised of self employed in poorly paid occupations, aged, unemployed, and extremely poor people in developing countries, who lack the protection of public safety net programs. Most developing countries are far away from the ILO's vision of universal social health protection coverage that aims to remove financial barriers preventing access to health services, and to protect people from the impoverishing effects of medical expenditures.

Even many developed countries, ranked highly in terms of economic and human development index, lack public-funding support programs for accessing life-saving medicines and for offsetting income loss during illness. Evidence shows that Australia, Canada, England, New Zealand, and Scotland have the most restricted access to publicly-funded cancer drugs (Cheema et al., 2012; Rawson, 2011; Rx&D International Report on Access to Medicines, 2010-2011). In dealing with the loss of income and productivity of a cancer patient or caregiver, gaps in public safety nets (as evident from the data on paid sick day and paid sick leave presented in Table 5), has remained a neglected issue in the public policy of most countries, particularly in Canada and the United States. Strengthening of the public safety net to provide income stability support to patients and caregivers during the treatment and recovery period requires urgent action.

Another alarming trend warranting attention is the steady increase of in-work poverty over the past decade in a number of OECD countries, where, on average in the mid-2000s, slightly more than one person in ten lived in a household with a disposable income below 50% of the median income in the OECD area (OECD, 2009). These working poor need better incomes, job security, and availability of regular health protection benefits such as those that are available in Nordic welfare states.

LMIC economies undergoing demographic and epidemiological transition face multiple challenges—some of the major challenges include higher cancer mortality rates, higher cancer drug prices relative to the per capita income level, low public funding for health care services resulting in heavy reliance on OOP expenses, and large numbers of citizens in the informal sector without the support of public pension or health care benefits throughout their lives. The unsustainability of cancer drug prices and accompanying access challenges have increased the need for government interventions to re-price drugs in consonance with the economic poverty level and treatment needs of the people. Differential pricing strategies are considered to be an economically justifiable policy option. To address the financial protection needs of people in low-income countries, ILO has recommended the implementation of national social protection floors containing basic social security guarantees that ensure universal access to essential health care and income security for all, at least at a nationally defined minimum level. Heavily populated countries like India and China are anticipated to face high burdens of non-communicable diseases in coming years. The present study has examined the initiatives taken in these countries toward implementation of the ILO's National Social Protection Floors (ILO Recommendation 2012, No. 202).

Comparing the performance of China and India in terms of social protection floors, China is observed to have outperformed India both in terms of extending health coverage and old age pension coverage to the population. In the case of legal health coverage, evidence shows that India falls under the category of developing countries where statutory health coverage—measured as proportion of the population covered by law—is below 50%, while China is bracketed among the category of nations where 75%–80% population has health coverage by law (OECD, 2011). In addition, China has made significant strides in pension coverage of its population, and by the end of 2013 nearly 75% of the population aged 15 and above was covered under the four pension schemes (ILO, 2014). Of the 20 developing countries that have universal pension coverage, Brazil and China have universal rural pension coverage (ILO, 2014). In India, under the Indira Gandhi National Old Age Pension scheme meant for the informal sector, only 19.1% of the population in the age group of 60 and above was covered by the non-contributory pension scheme in 2012 (ILO, 2014, 2015). India has launched many government programs, but many failed due to the inadequate prior study of the cost of programs

(International Social Security Association, 2013).

Despite strong evidence showing the positive contributions of social protection on individuals, households, and society, important social protection coverage gaps remain in many LMICs. The prominent challenges include impoverishing and catastrophic OOP expenses faced by people with chronic and long term ailments and meager provision for old age pension for poor in the informal sector, which can become further crippled by growing numbers of older people with NCDs.[69] Widespread unemployment and under-employment are additional contributory factors. In view of the above problems, policymakers and other stakeholders could consider progressing toward a more robust social protection system.

To contain the economic and social cost of cancer illness and reduce cancer deaths occurring without treatment in LMICs, international organizations (WHO, UN, Lancet) suggest increasing emphasis on cancer control measures—prevention, detection, screening, diagnosis, and palliative care (Gelband et al., 2016; WHO 2006-2007; UN 2015). Estimates have shown that more than 34% of cancer deaths are attributable to a small number of known modifiable risk factors (Abegunde, Mathers, Adam, Ortegon, & Strong, 2007). Liver cancer can be largely prevented with the hepatitis B vaccine. The prevention of cervical cancer is now possible with HPV vaccines (Beaglehole et al., 2011). Lifestyle changes such as controlling smoking and alcohol use, and cessation of tobacco chewing can prevent people from developing certain cancers (WHO, 2015). In LMICs where resources for treatment are already stretched to the limit, paying more attention to disease prevention programs to reduce known modifiable risk factors can serve as a cost-effective and resource-saving strategy.

As a concluding note, the following observations are worth reiterating. First, ground-breaking advances in immunotherapy, precision medicines, and prevention science herald a new era of diagnosing cancer diseases, inferring treatments, and developing new evidence-based drugs with less serious side effects (American Association for Cancer Research, 2014; Ginsburg & Willard, 2009). But rapid expedition of the journey from "bench to bedside" requires multiple initiatives at national and international levels. At the international level, open and integrated global collaboration is needed between hospitals and institutions to develop and share a big database relating to clinical, genomic, and proteomic data across a large population with diverse demographic characteristics. At the national level, government funding is indispensable in attaining rapid success in high-risk and pioneering cutting-edge research and in facilitating a new era of drug discovery. Public funded research also helps answer critical patient care questions that private industry research is unlikely to address (Dizon, 2016). All countries, particularly economically developed nations, need to make sustained efforts to generate robust funding for cancer research. Acceleration of the pace of research and discovery will help millions of affected people live a high quality of life (Dizon, 2016).

Another formidable challenge warranting immediate redress is to provide easy and affordable access of cutting-edge cancer treatment to all affected people and families with adequate public funding and social support. As Freeman (2004, P 77) has remarked, "To win the war against cancer, we must apply what we know at any given time to all people," including uninsured and underinsured. People in the lower socioeconomic strata in all countries face high odds of financial deprivation and social inequity in the access of required treatment due to their poor economic and employment status and their social exclusion. Incidentally, these socially disadvantaged people also face significantly higher risks of various types of cancer (Freeman, 2004; Merletti, Galassi, & Spadea et al., 2011; Gelband et al., 2016), and poorer cancer survival overall than higher social classes. In LMICs, a significant proportion of people outside the formal sector face immense risks of financial trauma due to economic poverty and ineligibility to social security benefits at the time of illness.

Policies are required that provide patients with effective access (timely, affordable, and cost-effective) to prescription drugs, shield them and their families against the disease related financial burden, while acknowledging the need for promoting R&D to support the advancement of knowledge and sustained development of new treatments.

References

Abegunde, D. O., Mathers, C. D., Adam, T., Ortegon, M., Strong, K. (2007). The burden and costs of chronic diseases in low-income and middle-income countries. The Lancet. 37, 1929–1938.

Alcohol and Cancer: A Statement of the American Society of Clinical Oncology Noelle K. LoConte, Abenaa M. Brewster, Judith S. Kaur, Janette K. Merrill, and Anthony J. Alberg 2018.

Alexander, B. M., Wen, P. Y., Trippa, L., Reardon, D. A., Yung, W. K. A., Parmigiani, G., & Berry, D. A. (2013). Biomarker-based adaptive trials for patients with glioblastoma—lessons from I-SPY 2.Neuro-Oncology. 15(8), 972–978. Retrieved from http://doi.org/10.1093/neuonc/not088.

American Cancer Society (2015), Global Cancer Facts and Figures 3rd edition https://www.cancer.org/content/dam/cancer-org/research/cancer-facts-and-statistics/global-cancer-facts-and-figures/global-cancer-facts-and-figures-3rd-edition.pdf

American Cancer Society Cancer Action Network. Out-of-pocket spending limits are crucial for cancer patients and survivors. Atlanta (GA): ACS CAN; 2017 Jan 9. Available from: https://www.acscan.org/sites/default/files/Maximum%20Out%20of%20Pocket%20Limits%20Fact-sheet%2001-06-17.pdf

American Association for Cancer Research. (2011). AACR Cancer Progress

Report 2011. Philadelphia, PA: American Association for Cancer Research.

American Association for Cancer Research. (2014). AACR Cancer Progress Report 2014. Philadelphia, PA: American Association for Cancer Research.

American Society of Clinical Oncology (2018): American Society of Clinical Oncology Position Statement on Addressing the Affordability of Cancer Drugs. J Oncol Pract. 2018 Mar;14(3):187-192.

American Cancer Society Cancer Action Network(2017): The Costs of Cancer, Addressing Patient Costs. https://www.acscan.org/policy-resources/costs-cancer.

Arrowsmith J., & Miller, P. (2013). Trial watch: phase II and phase III attrition rates 2011-2012. Nat. Rev. Drug Discov. 12:569. 10.1038/nrd4090 [PubMed].

de Arruda, P. L. (2015). Preliminary Observations on Social Security and Health Care Systems of the BRICS. Retrieved from The International Policy Centre for Inclusive Growth website: http://www.ipc-ndp.org/pub/eng/OP294_Preliminary_Observations_on_Social_Security_and_Health_Care_Systems_of_the_BRICS.pdf.

Aunan, J. R., Cho, W. C., & Søreide, K. (2017). The Biology of Aging and Cancer: A Brief Overview of Shared and Divergent Molecular Hallmarks. *Aging and disease*, 8(5), 628-642. doi:10.14336/AD.2017.0103

Aykan N. F. (2015). Red Meat and Colorectal Cancer. *Oncology reviews*, 9(1), 288. doi:10.4081/oncol.2015.288

Bach, P. B. (2009). Limits on Medicare's ability to control rising spending on cancer drugs. New England Journal of Medicine. 360(6), 626–633. Retrieved from http://doi.org/10.1056/NEJMhpr0807774.

Balducci L, Extermann M(2000). Management of cancer in the older person: a practical approach. Oncologist2000; 5: 224–237.

Bardia, A., & Baselga, J. (2013). Neoadjuvant therapy as a platform for drug development and approval in breast cancer. Clinical Cancer Research. 19(23), 6360–6370. Retrieved from http://doi.org/10.1158/1078-0432.CCR-13-0916.

Bates, S.E., Berry, D.A., Balasubramaniam, S., Bailey, S., LoRusso, P.M., & Rubin, E.H. (2015): Advancing Clinical Trials to Streamline Drug Development, Clin Cancer Res. 2015 Oct 15;21(20):4527-35. doi: 10.1158/1078-0432.CCR-15-0039.

Beaglehole, R., Bonita, R., Horton, R., Adams, C., Alleyne, G., Asaria, P., & Watt, J. (2011). Priority actions for the non-communicable disease crisis. The Lancet. 377(9775), 1438–1447. Retrieved from http://doi.org/10.1016/S0140–6736(11)60393–0.

Benach, J., Vives, A., Amable, M., Vanroelen, C., Tarafa, G., & Muntaner, C. (2014). Precarious employment: understanding an emerging social determinant of health. Annual Review of Public Health. 35, 229–253. Retrieved from http://doi.org/10.1146/annurev-publhealth-032013–182500.

Berger, N. A., Savvides, P., Koroukian, S. M., Kahana, E. F., Deimling, G. T., Rose, J. H., Bowman, K. F., … Miller, R. H. (2006). Cancer in the elderly. Transactions of the American Clinical and Climatological Association, 117, 147-55; discussion 155-6.

Berry, S. R., Evans, W. K., Strevel, E. L., & Bell, C. M. (2012). Variation and consternation: access to unfunded cancer drugs in Canada. Journal of Oncology Practice. 8(1), 35–39.

Bertagnolli, M. M., Canetta, R., & Nass, S. J. (2014). Expanding public-private collaborations to enhance cancer drug development: a report of the Institute of Medicine's workshop series, Implementing a National Cancer Clinical Trials System for the 21st Century. The Oncologist. 19(11), 1179–1185.

Bestvina, C. M., Zullig, L. L., & Yousuf Zafar, S. (2014). The implications of out-of-pocket cost of cancer treatment in the USA: a critical appraisal of the literature. Future Oncology. 10(14), 2189–2199.

Blackstone, E. A., & Fuhr, J. P. (2012). Innovation and Competition: Will Biosimilars Succeed?: The creation of an FDA approval pathway for biosimilars is complex and fraught with hazard. Yes, innovation and market competition are at stake. But so are efficacy and patient safety. Biotechnology healthcare, 9(1), 24-7.

Block G., Patterson B., Subar A. Fruit, vegetables, and cancer prevention(1992): A review of the epidemiological evidence. Nutr. Cancer. 1992;18:1–29

Block G, Patterson B, Subar A. Fruit, vegetables, and cancer prevention: a review of the epidemiological evidence. Nutr. Cancer. 1991;18(1):1–29; Ames, B. N., Shigenaga, M. K., & Hagen, T. M. (1993). Oxidants, antioxidants, and the degenerative diseases of aging. Proceedings of the National Academy of Sciences of the United States of America, 90(17), 7915-22.

Boldrin M, Levine DK(2013): The case against patents, Journal of Economic Perspectives, 2013, Vol. 27, No. 1, pp. 3-22

Bonter, K., Desjardins, C., Currier, N., Pun, J., & Ashbury, F. D. (2011). Personalised medicine in Canada: a survey of adoption and practice in oncology, cardiology and family medicine. BMJ Open. 1(1), e000110. Retrieved fromhttp://doi.org/10.1136/bmjopen-2011-000110.

Brady, D., Fullerton, A. S., & Cross, J. M. (2010). More than just nickels and dimes: a cross-national analysis of working poverty in affluent democracies. Social Problems. 57(4), 559–585.

Branzén, K. (2013): Personalized Medicine, a new era for healthcare and industry, life science foresight institute. Retrieved from http://ec.europa.eu/digital-agenda/futurium/sites/futurium/files/futurium/library/Branz%C3%A9n%20-%202013%20-%20Personalized%20Medicine(2).pdf.

Bray F, Ferlay J, Soerjomataram I, Siegel RL, Torre LA, Jemal A. Global Cancer Statistics 2018: GLOBOCAN Estimates of Incidence and Mortality Worldwide for 36 Cancers in 185 Countries. CA: a cancer journal for clinicians. 2018 Sep 12;

Bray F, Ferlay J, Laversanne M, Brewster DH, Gombe Mbalawa C, Kohler B, Pineros M, Steliarova-Foucher E, Swaminathan R, Antoni S, Soerjomataram I, Forman D. Cancer Incidence in Five Continents: Inclusion criteria, highlights from Volume X and the global status of cancer registration. Int J Cancer. 2015;137:2060–2071

Bray, F., Guilloux, A., Sankila, R. & Parkin, D.M. (2002) Practical implications of imposing a new World standard population. Cancer Causes Control, 13, 175–182

Bray F and Ferlay J(2019) International Agency for Cancer Research, Chapter 7: Age Standardization, Cancer Incidence in 5 continents, WHO, http://ci5.iarc.fr/CI5-XI/Pages/Chapter7.aspx

Brazas, M. D., Lewitter, F., Schneider, M. V., van Gelder, C. W. G, & Palagi, P. M. (2014). A quick guide to genomics and bioinformatics training for clinical and public audiences. PLoS computational biology. 10(4), e10035. Retrieved from http://doi.org/10.1371/journal.pcbi.1003510.

Brunt, L., Lerner, J., Nicholas, T., 2011. Inducement Prizes and Innovation. Harvard Business School, Boston: http://www.hbs.edu/faculty/Publication%20Files/11-118.pdf

Burke, W., Brown Trinidad, S., & Press, N. A. (2013). Essential elements of personalized medicine. Urologic oncology, 32(2), 193-7.

Cancer Advocacy Coalition of Canada. (2013). Report card on cancer in Canada, 2012–2013. Toronto, Ontario: Cancer Advocacy Coalition of Canada.

Canadian Cancer Society. (2012). Financial hardship for cancer: A call for action. Toronto, Canada: Canadian Cancer Society. Manitoba Division. Retrieved from http://stream1.newswire.ca/media/2012/11/01/20121101_C3870_DOC_EN_19977.pdf.

Cancer Information & Support Network (2006). How cancer is studied. Retrieved from http://cisncancer.org/research/how_cancer_is_studied/overview.html.

Canadian Institute of Health Information (2013) Health indicators 2013, Statistics Canada. Retrieved from https://secure.cihi.ca/free_products/HI2013_EN.pdf.

Cancer Research UK. (2014). Looking to the future: our strategy, in research strategy. London, UK: Cancer Research UK.

Cancer Research UK. (2016): Health economics: the cancer drugs cost conundrum https://www.cancerresearchuk.org/funding-for-researchers/research-features/2016-08-10-health-economics-the-cancer-drugs-cost-conundrum

Cancer Support Community(2016): Access to Care in Cancer2016, Barriers and Challenges A global network of education and hope

Carrera PM, Hagop MK, Blinder VS(2018): The financial burden and distress of patients with cancer: understanding and stepping-up action on the financial toxicity of cancer treatment. CA Cancer J. Clin. 2018;68:153–165.

Carter, J. L. (2014). New clinical trials designed to better leverage precision medicine. OBR Green 8(3). Retrieved from http://obroncology.com/obrgreen/article/New-Clinical-Trials-Designed-to-Better-Leverage-Precision-Medicine.

Carter, J. L., & Lokere, J. (2011). Personalized medicine, what is missing? Report Card on Cancer in Canada, 2010–2011.

Catenacci, D. V. T. (2015). Next-generation clinical trials: Novel strategies to address the challenge of tumor molecular heterogeneity. Molecular oncology. 9(5), 967–996.

Cerami, E., Gao, J., Dogrusoz, U., Gross, B. E., Sumer, S. O., Aksoy, B. A., Jacobsen, A. Byrne, C. J., Heuer, M. L., Larsson, E., Antipin, Y., Reva, B., Goldberg, A. P., Sander, C., & Schultz, N. (2012). The cBio cancer genomics portal: an open platform for exploring multidimensional cancer genomics data. Cancer Discovery. 2(5), 401–404.

Chandra, A., Jena, A. B., & Skinner, J. S. (2011). The pragmatist's guide to comparative effectiveness research. NBER Working Paper No. 16990 issued in April 2011 http://www.nber.org/papers/w16990.

Cheema, P. K., Gavura, S., Migus, M., Godman, B., Yeung, L., & Trudeau, M. E. (2012). International variability in the reimbursement of cancer drugs by publicly funded drug programs. Current Oncology, 19(3), e165–e176. http://doi.org/10.3747/co.19.946.

Chen H, Chiang R and Storey V(2012), "Business Intelligence and Analytics: From Big Data to Big Impact," MIS Quarterly, vol. 36 (4), pp. 1165-1188, 2012.

Chin, L., Andersen, J. L., & Futreal, P. A. (2011). Cancer genomics: from discovery science to personalized medicine. Nature medicine. 17(3), 297–303.

Clarke, J. M., Wang, X., & Ready, N. E. (2015). Surrogate clinical endpoints to predict overall survival in non-small cell lung cancer trials—are we in a new era? Translational lung cancer research. 4(6), 804.

Clarke, M. A., & Joshu, C. E. (2017). Early Life Exposures and Adult Cancer Risk. Epidemiologic reviews, 39(1), 11-27.

Cock, P., Antao, T., Chang, J. T., Chapman, B. A., Cox, C. J., Dalke, A., Friedberg, I., Hamelryck, T, Wilczynski, B., & de Hoon, M. J. (2009). Biopython: freely available Python tools for computational molecular biology and bioinformatics. Bioinformatics. 25(11), 1422–1423.

Cohn, J. (2004). Introduction to surrogate markers. Circulation 109(25 suppl 1), IV-20–IV-21.

Cohen D. (2017). Cancer drugs: high price, uncertain value. BMJ (Clinical research ed.), 359, j4543. doi:10.1136/bmj.j4543

Cohen DA, Richardson J, LaBree L(1994). Parenting behaviors and the onset of smoking and alcohol use: A longitudinal study. Pediatrics. 1994;94(3):368–375.

Cohen DA, Rice J(1997). Parenting styles, adolescent substance use, and academic achievement. J Drug Educ. 1997;27:199–211.

Coller, B. S., & Califf, R. M. (2009). Traversing the Valley of Death: A Guide to Assessing Prospects for Translational Success. Science Translational Medicine, 1(10), 10cm9. http://doi.org/10.1126/scitranslmed.3000265.

Commonwealth Fund. (2012). Young, uninsured and in debt: why young adults lack health insurance and how the affordable care act is helping. New York: Commonwealth Fund.

Cook-Deegan R. (2006). The science commons in health research: structure, function, and value. The Journal of technology transfer, 32, 133-156

Cressman, S., Browman, G. P., Hoch, J. S., Kovacic, L., & Peacock, S. J. (2015). A Time-Trend Economic Analysis of Cancer Drug Trials. The oncologist, 20(7), 729-36.

Dabla-Norris, E., Kochhar, K., Ricka, F., Suphaphiphat, N., & Tsounta, E. (2015). Causes and consequences of income inequality: A global perspective. IMF Staff Discussion Notes. 2015(13), 39.

Daley, C. A., Abbott, A., Doyle, P. S., Nader, G. A., & Larson, S. (2010). A review of fatty acid profiles and antioxidant content in grass-fed and grain-fed beef. Nutrition journal, 9, 10. doi:10.1186/1475-2891-9-10

Danzon, P. M., & Towse, A. (2003). Differential Pricing for Pharmaceuticals: Reconciling Access, R&D and Patents. International Journal of Health Care and Economics 3(3), 183-205.

Danzon, P. M., Towse, A., & Mulcahy, A. W. (2011). Setting cost-effectiveness thresholds as a means to achieve appropriate drug prices in rich and poor countries. Health affairs (Project Hope). 30(8), 1529–1538.

Danzon, P. M., Towse, A. & Mestre-Ferrandiz, J. (2013). Value-based differential pricing: efficient prices for drugs in a global context. Health Economics. [Online]. DOI: 10.1002/hec.3021.

Danzon P M and Taylor E (2010): Drug Pricing and Value in Oncology, The Oncologist 2010;15(suppl 1):24 –31

Davidoff, A. J., Erten, M., Shaffer, T., Shoemaker, J. S., Zuckerman, I. H., Pandya, N., Tai, M.H., Ke, X., & Stuart, B. (2013). Out-of-pocket health care expenditure burden for Medicare beneficiaries with cancer. Cancer. 119(6), 1257–1265. Retrieved from http://doi.org/10.1002/cncr.27848.

David Briggs; Environmental pollution and the global burden of disease, British Medical Bulletin, Volume 68, Issue 1, 1 December 2003, Pages 1–24, https://doi.org/10.1093/bmb/ldg019

Demetriou, C. A., & Vineis, P. (2015). Carcinogenicity of ambient air pollution: use of biomarkers, lessons learnt and future directions. Journal of thoracic disease, 7(1), 67-95.

de Martel C, Ferlay J, Franceschi S, Vignat J, Bray F, Forman D, Plummer M. Global burden of cancers attributable to infections in 2008: a review and synthetic analysis. Lancet Oncol. 2012;13:607–15.

Dieleman, J. L., Templin, T., Sadat, N., Reidy, P., Chapin, A., Foreman, K., Haakenstad, A., Evans, T., Murray, C., & Kurowski, C. (2016). National spending on health by source for 184 countries between 2013 and 2040. The Lancet. 387(10037), 2521–2535. Retrieved from http://dx.doi.org/10.1016/S0140-6736(16)30167-2.

Dieleman, J. L., Templin, T., Sadat, N., Reidy, P., Chapin, A., Foreman, K. Kurowski, C. (2016). National spending on health by source for 184 countries between 2013 and 2040. The Lancet. 387(10037), 2521–2535. http://dx.doi.org/10.1016/S0140-6736(16)30167-2

DiMasi, J., & Grabowski, H. G. (2007). Economics of new oncology drug development. Journal of Clinical Oncology. 25, 209–216.

DiMasi, J. A., Reichert, J. M., Feldman, L., & Malins, A. (2013). Clinical approval success rates for investigational cancer drugs. Clinical Pharmacology & Therapeutics. 94(3), 329–335.

Dizon, D. S., Krilov, L., Cohen, E., Gangadhar, T., Ganz, P. A., Hensing, T. A., Hunger, S., Krishnamurthi, S., Lassman, A., Markham, M., Mayer, E., Neuss, M., Kumar Pal, S., Richardson, L., Schilsky, R., Schwartz, G., Spriggs, D., Villalona-Calero, M. A., Villani, G., & Masters, G. (2016). Clinical Cancer Advances 2016: Annual Report on Progress against Cancer from the American Society of Clinical Oncology. Journal of Clinical Oncology: Official Journal of the American Society of Clinical Oncology, 34(9), 987–1011. http://doi.org/10.1200/JCO.2015.65.8427.

Docteur, E., & Paris, V. (2009). Ensuring efficiency in pharmaceutical expenditures, in achieving better value for money in health care. Retrieved from OECD Publishing, Paris. http://dx.doi.org/10.1787/9789264074231-5-en.

Doll R, Peto R(1981). The causes of cancer: quantitative estimates of avoidable risks of cancer in the United States today. J Natl Cancer Inst. 1981;66(6):1191–1308

Dragsted LO, Strube M, Larsen JC.(1993) Cancer-protective factors in fruits and vegetables: Biochemical and biological background. Pharmacol Toxicol. 1993;72:116–135.

Eddy D M (1986). Secondary prevention of cancer: an overview. Bulletin of the World Health Organization, 64(3), 421-9.

Edwards A(2008). Open-source science to enable drug discovery. Drug Discov Today 2008;13:731–3

Eichler, H. G., Oye, K., Baird, L. G., Abadie, E., Brown, J., Ferguson, J., &

Garner, S. (2012). Adaptive licensing: taking the next step in the evolution of drug approval. Clinical pharmacology & therapeutics. 91(3), 426.

Eisenstein, M. (2014). Clinical trials: more trials, fewer tribulations. Scientific American. 311(1), 109–111.

Epstein LH, Gordy CC, Raynor HA, Beddome M, Kilanowski CK, Paluch R.(2001) Increasing fruit and vegetable intake and decreasing fat and sugar intake in families at risk for childhood obesity. Obes Res2001;9(3):171–8. 10.1038/oby.2001.18

Evans, D. B., Elovainio, R., & Humphreys, G. (2010). Health systems financing: the path to universal coverage, in the world health report. Geneva, Switzerland: World Health Organization.

Experts in Chronic Myeloid Leukemia (2013). The price of drugs for chronic myeloid leukemia (CML) is a reflection of the unsustainable prices of cancer drugs: from the perspective of a large group of CML experts. Blood, 121(22), 4439-42

Fenn, K. M., Evans, S. B., McCorkle, R., DiGiovanna, M.P., Pusztai, L., Sanft, T., Hofstatter, E., Killelea, B., Knobf, T., Lannin, D., Maysa, A., Horowitz, N., & Chagpar, A. (2014). Impact of financial burden of cancer on survivors' quality of life? Journal of Oncology Practice. 10(5), 332-338.

Ferlay, J., Shin, H.R., Bray, F., Forman, D., Mathers, C., Parkin, D.M. (2010). Estimates of worldwide burden of cancer in 2008: GLOBOCAN 2008. Int J Cancer; 127:2893–2917.

Ferlay, J. Soerjomataram, R., Dikshit, S., Eser, C., Mathers, M., Rebelo, D.M., Parkin, D., Forman, D., Bray, F. (2014). Cancer incidence and mortality worldwide: sources, methods and major patterns in GLOBOCAN 2012. International Journal of Cancer doi:10.1002/ijc.29210 PMID:25220842 Published online 9 October 2014

Ferlay J, Soerjomataram I, Dikshit R, Eser S, Mathers C, Rebelo M, et al. Cancer incidence and mortality worldwide: Sources, methods and major patterns in GLOBOCAN 2012. Int J Cancer2015;136(5):E359–86. doi: 10.1002/ijc.29210.

Frank RG(2007): The Ongoing Regulation of Generic Drugs, New England Journal of Medicine • December 2007

Freeman, H. P. (2004). Poverty, Culture, and Social Injustice Determinants of Cancer Disparities, CA Cancer J Clin 2004;54:72–77, http://onlinelibrary.wiley.com/doi/10.3322/canjclin.54.2.72/pdf.

Free radicals, antioxidants in disease and health. International journal of biomedical science : IJBS, 4(2), 89-96.

Fitzmaurice, C., Allen, C., Barber, R. M., Barregard, L., Bhutta, Z. A., et al. (2017): Global, regional, and national cancer incidence, mortality, years of life lost, years lived with disability, and disability-adjusted life-years for 32 cancer groups, 1990 to 2015: a systematic analysis for the global burden of disease study. JAMA Oncol.3, 524–548. Global Burden of Disease Cancer Collaboration

Gaffney, A. (2014). EMA unveils new adaptive licensing initiative, meant to provide earlier niche approvals. Retrieved from http://www.raps.org/focus-online/news/news-article-view/article/4794/.

Gagnon, M. & Hébert, G. (2010). The Economic Case for Universal Pharmacare. Costs and Benefits of Publicly Funded Drug Coverage for all Canadians. Canadian Centre for Policy Alternatives and Institute de recherché et d'informations socio-économiques. 1-86, ISBN 978-1-926888-13-2.

Garber, A. M. (2008). A menu without prices. Annals of internal medicine. 148(12), 964–966.

Garrison, L. P. (2010). Rewarding value creation to promote innovation in oncology: the importance of considering the global product life cycle. The Oncologist. 15 (suppl 1).

Gelband, H., Sankaranarayanan, R., Gauvreau, C. L., Horton, S., Anderson, B.O., Bray, F., Cleary, J., Dare, A. J., Denny, L., Gospodarowicz, M. K., Gupta, S., Howard, S. C., Jaffray, D. A., Knaul, F., Levin, C., Rabeneck, L., Rajaraman, P., Sullivan, T., Trimble, E.L., & Jha, P. for the Disease Control Priorities-3 Cancer Author Group (2016): Costs, affordability, and feasibility of an essential package of cancer control interventions in low-income and middle-income countries: Key messages from Disease

Control Priorities, 3rd edition. Lancet. 2015. Published online Lancet 2016; 387:2133-44.

Gentleman, R. C., Carey, V. J., Bates, D. M., Bolstad, B., Dettling, M., Dudoit, S., Ellis, B., Gautier, L., Ge, Y., Gentry, J., Hornik, K., Hothorn, T., Huber, W., Iacus, S., Irizarry, R., Leisch, F., Li, C., Maechler, M., Rossini, A. J., Sawitzki, G., Smith, C., Smyth, G., Tierney, L., Yang, J. Y., &Zhang J. (2004). Bioconductor: open software development for computational biology and bioinformatics. Genome Biology. 5(10), 1–16.

Ginsburg, G. S. & Willard, H. F. (2009): Genomic and personalized medicine: foundations and applications. Transl Res. 2009 Dec;154(6):277-87. doi: 10.1016/j.trsl.2009.09.005. Epub 2009 Oct 1.

Glanz K. Yaroch AL(2004). Strategies for increasing fruit and vegetable intake in grocery stores and communities: policy, pricing, and environmental change. Prev Med. 2004;39:75–80

Global Burden of Disease Cancer Collaboration. Fitzmaurice C., Dicker D., Pain A., Hamavid H., Moradi-Lakeh M., et al. (2015). The global burden of cancer 2013. JAMA Oncol. 1 505–527. 10.1001/jama-oncol.2015.0735

Global Burden of Disease Cancer Collaboration, Fitzmaurice C, Dicker D, et al. The Global Burden of Cancer 2013. JAMA Oncol. 2015;1(4):505-27.

Global Burden of Disease Cancer Collaboration, (2015). The global burden of cancer 2013. Retrieved from JAMA Oncology. 1(4), 505–527 http://doi.org/10.1001/jamaoncol.2015.0735.

Gold, E. R., Kaplan, W., Orbinski, J., Harland-Logan, S., & N-Marandi, S. (2010). Are Patents Impeding Medical Care and Innovation? PLOS Medicine 7(1): e1000208. https://doi.org/10.1371/journal.pmed.1000208.

Goldstein, D. A., Chen, Q., Ayer, T., Chan, K., Virik, K., Hammerman, A., Brenner, B., Flowers, C. R., … Hall, P. S. (2017). Bevacizumab for Metastatic Colorectal Cancer: A Global Cost-Effectiveness Analysis. The oncologist, 22(6), 694-699.

Gonzalez-Angulo, A. A., Hennessy, B., & Mills, G. B. (2010). Future of personalized medicine in oncology: a systems biology approach. Journal of Clinical Oncology. 28(16), 2777–2783.

Goss, P. E., Strasser-Weippl, K., Lee-Bychkovsky, B. L., Fan, L., Li, J., ChavarriGuerra, Y., Liedke, P. E., Pramesh, C. S., Badovinac-Crnjevic, T., Sheikine, Y. (2014). Challenges to effective cancer control in China, India, and Russia. Lancet Oncol.;15(5):489–538.

Grootendorst, P., Hollis, A., Levine, D. K., Pogge, T., & Edwards, A. M. (2011). New approaches to rewarding pharmaceutical innovation. Canadian Medical Association Journal. 183(6), 681–685.

Gruber, Jonathan. (2008). Incremental universalism for the United States: the states move first? The Journal of Economic Perspectives. 22(5), 51–68.

Gruber, J. (2010). Health care reform is a 'three-legged stool:' the cost of partially repealing the affordable care act. Retrieved from https://www.americanprogress.org/issues/healthcare/reports/2010/08/05/8226/health-care-reform-is-a-three-legged-stool/.

Gruber, J. (2011). Massachusetts points the way to successful health care reform. Journal of Policy Analysis and Management. 30(1), 184–192.

Gyawali B. (2017). Cancer drugs in LMICs: cheap but unaffordable. Oncotarget, 8(52), 89425-89426. doi:10.18632/oncotarget.21976

Hamburg, M. A., & Collins, F. S. (2010). The path to personalized medicine. New England Journal of Medicine. 363(4), 301–304.

Hay, M., Thomas, D.W., Craighead, J. L., Economides, C., & Rosenthal, J. (2014). Clinical development success rates for investigational drugs. Nature Biotechnology. 32(1), 40–51.

Heller, M., & Eisenberg, R. (1998a). Can patents deter innovation? The anticommons in biomedical research. Science, 280, 698–701.

Heller, M. A. & Eisenberg, R. S. (1998b). "Upstream Patents = Downstream Bottlenecks Law Quad." Notes 41, no. 3 (1998): 93-7. (Excerpted from "Can Patents Deter Innovation? The Anticommons in Biomedical Research." Science 280, no. 5364.

Heller, M. (2010): The Tragedy of Anticommons, the Wealth of the Commons. A World beyond Market and Sate. This essay is adapted from Chapter 2 of The Gridlock Economy (2010). For further resources, see http://www.gridlockeconomy.com.

Hendren, S., Chin, N., Fisher, S., Winters, P., Griggs, J., Mohile, S., & Fiscella, K. (2011). Patients' barriers to receipt of cancer care, and factors associated with needing more assistance from a patient navigator. Journal of the National Medical Association, 103(8), 701-10.

Heymann, J., Rho, H. J., Schmitt, J., & Earle, A. (2009). Contagion nation: a comparison of paid sick day policies in 22 countries. Washington, DC: Center for Economic and Policy Research.

Heymann, J., Rho, H. J., Schmitt, J., & Earle, A. (2010). Ensuring a healthy and productive workforce: comparing the generosity of paid sick day and sick leave policies in 22 countries. International Journal of Health Services. 40(1), 1–22.

Hobin, J. A., Deschamps, A. M., Bockman, R., Cohen, S., Dechow, P., Eng, C., Galey, W., Morris, M., Prabhakar, S., Raj, U., Rubenstein, P., Smith, J., Stover, P., Sung, N., Talman, W., & Galbraith, R. (2012). Engaging basic scientists in translational research: identifying opportunities, overcoming obstacles. Journal of Translational Medicine, 10, 72. http://doi.org/10.1186/1479-5876-10-72.

Hollis, A. (2004a). An Efficient Reward System for Pharmaceutical Innovation. Unpublished Manuscript, Department of Economics, University of Calgary.

Hollis A(2004b): Me-too drugs: is there a problem, WHO Report, 2004/12/13, https://www.who.int/intellectualproperty/topics/ip/Me-tooDrugs_Hollis1.pdf

Hollis, A. (2008). The health impact fund: a useful supplement to the patent system? Public Health Ethics. 1(2), 124–133.

Hopkins, R. B., Goeree, R., & Longo, C. J. (2010). Estimating the national wage loss from cancer in Canada. Current Oncology. 17(2), 40–49.

Howard, D. H., Bach, P. B., Berndt, E. R., & Conti, R. M. (2015). Pricing in the market for anticancer drugs. Journal of Economic Perspectives. 29(1), 139–62.

Hotez, P. J., Cohen, R., Mimura, C., Yamada, T., & Hoffman, S. L. (2013). Strengthening mechanisms to prioritize, coordinate, finance, and execute R&D to meet health needs in developing countries. Retrieved from Washington, DC: Institute of Medicine. http://nam.edu/wp-content/uploads/2015/06/StrengtheningMechanismsRD.

Husereau, D. R., & Cameron, C. G. (2011). Value-Based Pricing of Pharmaceuticals in Canada: Opportunities to Expand the Role of Health Technology Assessment? Ottawa, Ontario: Canadian Health Services Research Foundation.

Hutchinson, L., & Kirk, R. (2011). High drug attrition rates—where are we going wrong? Nature Reviews. Clinical Oncology. 8(4), 189–190.

International Labour Organization. (2008). Social health protection. An ILO strategy towards universal access to health care, In Social security policy briefings. Geneva, Switzerland: International Labour Organization.

International Labour Organization (2012): Statistical update on employment in the informal economy. Retrieved from International Labour Organization - Department of Statistics June 2012, http://laborsta.ilo.org/informal_economy_E.html.

International Labour Organization. (2014a). Global employment trends 2014: risk of a jobless recovery? Geneva, Switzerland: International Labour Organization.

International Labour Organization. (2014b). World social protection report 2014/2015, building economic recovery, inclusive development and social justice. Geneva, Switzerland: International Labour Organization.

International Labour Organization & Organisation for Economic Co-operation and Development. (2011). Towards national protection floors, a policy note for the G20 meeting of labor and employment ministers. Paris: International Labour Organization & Organisation for Economic Co-operation and Development.

International Labor Organization & Organisation for Economic Co-operation and Development. (2015). The labour share in G20 economies. Report prepared for the G20 Employment Working Group.

ILO (2017): Fiscal Space for Social Protection and the SDGs: Options to Expand Social Investments in 187 Countries / Isabel Ortiz, Matthew Cummins, Kalaivani Karunanethy; International Labour Office. - Geneva: ILO, 2017

ILO Press Release(2018): Informal economy :More than 60 per cent of the world's employed population are in the informal economy,

International Social Security Association. (2013). Social security coverage extension in the BRICS a comparative study on the extension of coverage in Brazil, the Russian Federation, India, China. Geneva, Switzerland: International Social Security Association.

IMS Institute for Healthcare Informatics. (2014). Medicine use and shifting costs of healthcare: A review of the use of medicines in the United States in 2013. Danbury, CT: IMS Institute for Healthcare Informatics

IOM (Institute of Medicine). 2013. Delivering high-quality cancer care: Charting a new course for a system in crisis. Washington, DC: The National Academies Press

IOM (Institute of Medicine). 2014. Ensuring patient access to affordable cancer drugs: Workshop summary. Washington, DC: The National Academies Press.

Irwin, M. L., McTiernan, A., Baumgartner, R. N., Baumgartner, K. B., Bernstein, L., Gilliland, F. D., & Ballard-Barbash, R. (2005). Changes in body fat and weight after a breast cancer diagnosis: influence of demographic, prognostic, and lifestyle factors. Journal of clinical oncology : official journal of the American Society of Clinical Oncology, 23(4), 774-82.

Jacobsen, P. B., & Andrykowski, M. A. (2015). Tertiary prevention in cancer care: Understanding and addressing the psychological dimensions of cancer during the active treatment period. American Psychologist, 70(2), 134-145.

JAMA Oncol. 2017;3(4):524-548. Global Burden of Disease Cancer Collaboration.

Jayadev A, Stiglitz J.(2009 Two ideas to increase innovation and reduce pharmaceutical costs and prices. Health Aff 2009;28: w165–8

Jemal, A., Bray, F., Center, M. M., Ferlay, J., Ward, E., & Forman, D. (2011).

Global cancer statistics. CA: A Cancer Journal for Clinicians. 61(2), 69–90.

Jemal A, Bray F, Center MM, Ferlay J, Ward E, Forman D. Global cancer statistics. CA Cancer J Clin. 2011;61:69–90. doi: 10.3322/caac.20107

Jemal, A., Thun, M. J., Ries, L. A., Howe, H. L., Weir, H. K., Center, M. M., Ward, E., Wu, X. C., Eheman, C., Anderson, R., Ajani, U. A., Kohler, B., … Edwards, B. K. (2008). Annual report to the nation on the status of cancer, 1975-2005, featuring trends in lung cancer, tobacco use, and tobacco control. Journal of the National Cancer Institute, 100(23), 1672-94.

Johnson, J. K. M. &Williamson, J. B. (2008). Universal non-contributory pension schemes for low-income countries: An assessment. In: Kemp PA, Bosch K, Smith L, eds. Social protection in an aging world, International Series on Social Security, Volume 13. Antwerp Belgium, Intersentia.

Jones, G. H., Carrier, M. A., Silver, R. T., & Kantarjian, H. (2016). Strategies that delay or prevent the timely availability of affordable generic drugs in the United States. Blood, 127(11), 1398-402.

Kaitin, K.I., & DiMasi, J. A. (2011). Pharmaceutical innovation in the 21st century: New drug approvals in the first decade, 2000–2009. Clinical Pharmacology & Therapeutics. 89(2), 183–188.

Kale HP, Carroll NV.(2016) Self-reported financial burden of cancer care and its effect on physical and mental health-related quality of life among US cancer survivors. Cancer. 2016;122:283–289. doi: 10.1002/cncr.29808

Kalia, M. (2013). Personalized oncology: recent advances and future challenges. Metabolism. 62, S11-S14.

Kanavos P(2006). The rising burden of cancer in the developing world. Ann Oncol. 2006; 17:viii15–viii23.

Kankeu, H. T., Saksena, P., Xu, K., & Evans, D. B. (2013). The financial burden from non-communicable diseases in low and middle-income countries: a literature review. Health Research Policy and Systems. 11, 31.

Kantarjian, H. M., Fojo, T., Mathisen, M., & Zwelling. L. A. (2013). Cancer drugs in the United States: justum pretium—the just price. Journal of clinical oncology. 31(28), 3600–3604.

Kantarijan, H., Steensma, D., Rius Sanjuan, J., Elshaug, A., and Light, D. High cancer drug prices in the United States: reasons and proposed solutions. J Oncol Pract. 2014; 10: e208–e21

Kantarjian Hagop, Rajkumar S Vincent (2015). Why are cancer drugs so expensive in the United States, and what are the solutions? *Mayo Clinic proceedings.* 2015;90:500–504.

Kapsalis, C., & Tourigny, P. (2004). Duration of non-standard employment. Perspectives on Labour and Income. 5(12), 5–13.

Key TJ, Schatzkin A, Willett WC, Allen NE, Spencer EA, Travis RC(2004). Diet, nutrition and the prevention of cancer. Public Health Nutr. 2004;7:187–200.

Khanna I.(2012): Drug discovery in pharmaceutical industry: productivity challenges and trends. Drug Discovery Today. 2012; Oct;17(19-20):1088-102.

Khoury, M. J., Gwinn, M., Yoon, P. W., Dowling, N., Moore, C. A., & Bradley, L. (2007). The continuum of translation research in genomic medicine: how can we accelerate the appropriate integration of human genome discoveries into health care and disease prevention? Genetics in Medicine. 9(10), 665–674.

Kim, E. S., Herbst, R. S., Wistuba, I. I., Lee, J. J., Blumenschein, G. R., Tsao, A., Stewart, D., Hicks, M., Erasmus, J., Gupta S., Alden, C., Liu, S., Tang, X., Khuri, F., Tran, H., Johnson, B., Heymach, J., Mao, L., Fossella, F., Kies, M., Papadimitrakopoulou, V., Davis, S., Lippman, S., & Hong, W. 2011. The BATTLE trial: personalizing therapy for lung cancer. Cancer discovery. 1(1), 44–53.

Kirschner, N., Pauker, S. G., Stubbs, J. W. (2008). Information on Cost-Effectiveness: An Essential Product of a National Comparative Effectiveness Program. Annals of Internal Medicine. 148(12)956-61.

Kluetz, P., & Donoghue, M. (2014). FDA programs to expedite drug and biologic product development. Retrieved from A Conversation with FDA's Office of Hematology and Oncology Products, http://www.ascopost.com/issues/february-15–2014/fda-programs-to-expedite-drug-

and-biologic-product-development/.

Knaul, F. M., González-Pier, E., Gómez-Dantés, O., García-Junco, D., Arreola-Ornelas, H., Barraza-Lloréns, M., Sandoval, R., Caballero, F., Hernández-Avila, M., Juan, M., Kershenobich, D., Nigenda, G., Ruelas, E., Sepúlveda, J., Tapia, R., Soberón, G., Chertorivski, S. &Frenk, J. (2012). The quest for universal health coverage: achieving social protection for all in Mexico. The Lancet. 380(9849), 1259–1279.

Kola, I., & Landis, J. (2004). Can the pharmaceutical industry reduce attrition rates? Nature reviews. Drug discovery. 3(8), 711–716.

Kremer, Michael, and Heidi Williams. 2009. “Incentivizing Innovation: Adding to the Toolkit.” In Innovation Policy and the Economy, Vol. 10, edited by Josh Lerner and Scott Stern, 1–17. Chicago University Press.

Kriebel D, Hoppin PJ, Jacobs MM. Environmental and economic strategies for primary prevention of cancer in early life. Pediatrics. 2016;138(suppl 1)

Kumar H, Fojo T, Mailankody S: An appraisal of clinically meaningful outcomes guidelines for oncology clinical trials. JAMA Oncol 2:1238-1240, 2016

Kumthekar, P., Stell, B. V., Jacobs, D. I., Helenowski, I. B., Rademaker, A. W., Grimm, S. A., Bennett, C.L., & Raizer, J. J. (2014). Financial burden experienced by patients undergoing treatment for malignant gliomas. Neuro-Oncology Practice, 1(2), 71–76. http://doi.org/10.1093/nop/npu002.

Kutzin J (2012). Anything goes on the path to universal health coverage? No. In: WHO, editor. Bull World Health Organ, vol. 90. 2012. p. 867–8.

Lacombe. D. A (2014): Can collaborative molecular screening platforms (CMSPS) support new forms of cancer clinical research? The example of the EORTC SPECTA programme. Annals of Oncology 25(suppl 4): iv41. doi:10.1093/annonc/mdu317.3.

Landrigan, P. J., Schechter, C. B., Lipton, J. M., Fahs, M. C., & Schwartz, J. (2002). Environmental pollutants and disease in American children: estimates of morbidity, mortality, and costs for lead poisoning, asthma, cancer, and developmental disabilities. Environmental health perspectives, 110(7), 721-8.

de Lartigue, J. (2014). A look at I-SPY 2: Novel Trial Design May Expand the Scope of Oncology Drug Development. Retrieved from Oncology Drug Development 2016 (Wednesday April 2 2014). http://www.onclive.com/publications/oncology-live/2014/march-2014/a-look-at-i-spy-2-novel-trial-design-may-expand-the-scope-of-oncology-drug-development.

Law Commission of Ontario. (2012). Vulnerable Workers and Precarious Work. Toronto: Law Commission of Ontario.

Lenguaer, C., Diaz, L. A., & Saha, S. (2005). Cancer drug discovery through collaboration. Nature Reviews. Drug Discovery. 4(5), 375–380.

Li, Y. Y., & Jones, S. J. (2012). Drug repositioning for personalized medicine. Genome Medicine, 4(3), 27. http://doi.org/10.1186/gm326.

Light, D. W., & Lexchin, J. R. (2012). Pharmaceutical research and development: what do we get for all that money? BMJ. 345, e4348.

Lock, K., Pomerleau, J., Causer, L., Altmann, D. R., & McKee, M. (2005). The global burden of disease attributable to low consumption of fruit and vegetables: implications for the global strategy on diet. Bulletin of the World Health Organization, 83(2), 100-8.

Lohmann, H., Frauke, Peter., Rostgaard, T., &Spiess, K. (2009). Towards a Framework for Assessing Family Policies in the EU. OECD Social, Employment and Migration Working Papers, No. 88, OECD Publishing, Paris. Retrieved from DOI: http://dx.doi.org/10.1787/223883627348.

Longo, C. J., Fitch, M., Deber, R. B., & Williams, A. P. (2006). Financial and family burden associated with cancer treatment in Ontario, Canada. Supportive Care in Cancer. 14(11), 1077–1085.

Longo, C. J., & Bereza, B. G. (2011). A comparative analysis of monthly out-of-pocket costs for patients with breast cancer as compared with other common cancers in Ontario, Canada. Current Oncology, 18(1), e1–e8.

Lopert, R., Lang, D., Hill, S., & Henry, D. (2002). Differential pricing of drugs: a role for cost effectiveness analysis? The Lancet. 359, 2105-2107.

Love, J. (2011). Will the UN backtrack on accessible medicine? Retrieved from http://www.aljazeera.com/indepth/opinion/2011/09/20119149271427949 3.html.

Love, J., & Hubbard, T. (2007). The Big Idea: Prizes to Stimulate R&D for New Medicines. Chicago-Kent Law Review. 82(3), 1519-1554.

Love J (2012): Balancing Options for health research and development. Bulletin of the World Health Organization, 90, 796-796A

Luengo-Fernandez R, Leal J, Gray A, Sullivan R.(2013): Economic burden of cancer across the European Union: a population-based cost analysis. Lancet Oncol. 2013;14: 1165–1174.

Luo J, Hendryx M, and Ducatman A(2011), Association between Six Environmental Chemicals and Lung Cancer Incidence in the United States, Journal of Environmental and Public Health, vol. 2011, Article ID 463701, 9 pages, 2011. https://doi.org/10.1155/2011/463701.

Mak K, Kum CK. How to appraise a prognostic study. World J Surg. 2005;29:567-569.

Mandelblatt, J. S., Ramsey, S. D., Lieu, T. A., & Phelps, C. E. (2017). Evaluating Frameworks That Provide Value Measures for Health Care Interventions. Value in health : the journal of the International Society for Pharmacoeconomics and Outcomes Research, 20(2), 185-192.

Mariotto, A. B., Yabroff, K. R., Shao, Y., Feuer, E. J., & Brown, M. L. (2011). Projections of the cost of cancer care in the United States: 2010-2020. Journal of the National Cancer Institute, 103(2), 117-28.

McIntyre, D., & Meheus, F. (2014). Fiscal space for domestic funding of health and other social services. London: Chatham House.

Mellace, J. (2010). The financial burden of cancer care. Social Work Today, Vol. 10 No. 2 P. 14. Retrieved from http://www.socialworktoday.com/archive/032210p14.shtml.

Meng, Q., Fang, H., Liu, X., Yuan, B., & Xu, J. (2015). Consolidating the social health insurance schemes in China: towards an equitable and efficient health system. The Lancet. 386(10002), 1484–1492.

Menis, J., Hasan, B., & Besse, B. (2014). New clinical research strategies in thoracic oncology: Clinical trial design, adaptive, basket and umbrella trials, new end-points and new evaluations of response. European Respiratory Review. 23(133), 367–378.

Merletti, F., Galassi, C., & Spadea, T. (2011). The socioeconomic determinants of cancer. Environmental Health, 10(Suppl 1), S7. http://doi.org/10.1186/1476-069X-10-S1-S7.

Meslin, E. M., Blasimme, A., & Cambon-Thomsen, A. (2013). Mapping the translational science policy "valley of death." Clinical and Translational Medicine, 2, 14. http://doi.org/10.1186/2001-1326-2-14.

Moon, S., Bermudez, J., &'tHoen, E. (2012). Innovation and Access to Medicines for Neglected Populations: Could a Treaty Address a Broken Pharmaceutical R&D ystem? PLoS Medicine, 9(5), e1001218. http://doi.org/10.1371/journal.pmed.1001218.

Moreno-Serra, R., Millett, C., & Smith, P. C. (2011). Towards improved measurement of financial protection in health. PLoS Medicine. 8(9), 1166.

Moreno L., Pearson A.D. How can attrition rates be reduced in cancer drug discovery? Expert Opin. Drug Discov. 2013;8:363–368. doi: 10.1517/17460441.2013.768984

Morgan, S., Daw, J., & Law, M. R. (2013). Rethinking pharmacare in Canada. Toronto: CD Howe Institute.

National Cancer Policy Forum; Board on Health Care Services, Institute of Medicine. Ensuring Patient Access to Affordable Cancer Drugs: Workshop Summary. National Academies Press; Washington, DC, USA: 2014.

National Academic Press 2011: National Research Council (US) Committee to Study the National Needs for Biomedical, Behavioral, and Clinical Research Personnel. Research Training in the Biomedical, Behavioral, and Clinical Research Sciences. Washington (DC): National Academies Press (US); 2011. 3, Basic Biomedical Sciences. Available from: https://www.ncbi.nlm.nih.gov/books/NBK56989

Narayanan DL, Saladi RN, Fox JL. Ultraviolet radiation and skin cancer. Int J Dermatol. 2010;49(9):978–986. [Jemal A., Bray F., Center M., Ferlay J., Ward E., Forman D., "Global cancer statistics," CA: Cancer J. Clin.

61, 69–90 (2011).

Nathan C. Aligning pharmaceutical innovation with medical need. Nat Med. 2007;13:304–308

OECD. (2009). Achieving Better Value for Money in Health Care. OECD Health Policy Studies, Ch 4, Ensuring Efficiency in Pharmaceutical Expenditures. Retrieved from http://www.keepeek.com/Digital-Asset-Management/oecd/social-issues-migration-health/achieving-better-value-for-money-in-health-care_9789264074231-en#page1 ISBN: 978-92-6407423-1 (PDF).

Offit, K. (2011). Personalized medicine: new genomics, old lessons. Human genetics. 130(1), 3–14.

Organisation for Economic Co-operation and Development. (2015). In it together: why less inequality benefits all. Paris: Organisation for Economic Co-operation and Development. Retrieved from http://doi.org/10.1787/9789264235120-en.

OECD (2018): Pharmaceutical Innovation and Access to Medicines

Palmer, W. N. (2013). Global trends in pharmaceutical pricing and reimbursement in Canada [PowerPoint Slides]. Retrieved from http://pdci.ca/pdf/events/Palmer-Presentation-EyeforPharma-(October%2028,2013).pdf.

Pammolli, F., Magazzini, L., & Riccaboni, M. (2011). The productivity crisis in pharmaceutical R&D. Nature Reviews Drug Discovery. 10(6), 428–438.

Paris, V. and Docteur, E. (2006). Pharmaceutical pricing and reimbursement policies in Canada. OECD Health Working Paper, No. 24, OECD Publishing, Paris.

Parkin DM. Global cancer statistics in the year 2000. Lancet Oncol. (2001) 2:533–43. 10.1016/S1470-2045(01)00486-7

Parkin D, Pisani P, Ferlay J. Estimates of the worldwide incidence of eighteen major cancers in 1985. Int J Cancer. 1993;54:594–606

Patel. V., Parikh. R., Nandraj. S., Balasubramaniam. P., Narayan. K., Paul. V. K., Shiva Kumar, A. K., Chatterjee, M., & Reddy, K. S. (2015). Assuring health coverage for all in India. The Lancet. 386 (10011), 2422–

2435.

Paul, S. M., Mytelka, D. S., Dunwiddie, C. T., Persinger, C. C., Munos, B. H., Lindborg, S. R., & Schacht, A. L. (2010). How to improve R&D productivity: the pharmaceutical industry's grand challenge. Nature Reviews. Drug Discovery. 9(3), 203–214.

Pazdur, R. (2008). Endpoints for assessing drug activity in clinical trials. The Oncologist. 13(suppl 2), 19–21.

Perera F(1993): Prevention of Environmental Pollution: Good for Our Health, Editorial, Environmental Health Perspectives Volume 101, Number 7, December 1993

Peres, J. (2014). Neoadjuvant trials could speed up drug approvals. Journal of the National Cancer Institute. 106(3), dju072. Retrieved from http://jnci.oxfordjournals.org/content/early/2014/03/06/jnci.dju072.full.

Petersen PE. Oral cancer prevention and control – The approach of the World Health Organization. Oral Oncol. 2009;45:454–60.

Petrie J, Bunn F, Byrne G. (2006) Parenting programmes for preventing tobacco, alcohol or drugs misuse in children < 18: a systematic review. Health Educ Res. 2006;22(2):177–191

Plummer M, Martel C de, Vignat J, Ferlay J, Bray F, Franceschi S. Global burden of cancers attributable to infections in 2008: a review and synthetic analysis. Lancet Glob Heal. The Lancet; 2016;4(9):e609–16. 10.1016/S2214-109X(16)30143-7 [PubMed] [CrossRef]

Plummer M, de Martel C, Vignat J, Ferlay J, Bray F, Franceschi S. Global burden of cancers attributable to infections in 2012: a synthetic analysis. Lancet Glob Health. 2016;4:609–616. doi: 10.1016/S2214-109X(16)30143-7

Poljsak, B., Šuput, D., & Milisav, I. (2013). Achieving the balance between ROS and antioxidants: when to use the synthetic antioxidants. Oxidative medicine and cellular longevity, 2013, 956792.

Poljsak B and Milisav I (2013b) Aging, Oxidative Stress and Antioxidants, INTECH, Open Science, Ch 14, http://dx.doi.org/10.5772/51609

President's Council of Advisors on Science and Technology. (2012). Report to the President on Propelling Innovation in Drug Discovery, Development, and Evaluation. Washington, DC: President's Council of Advisors on Science and Technology.

President's Cancer Panel (2018): Promoting Value, Affordability, and Innovation in Cancer Drug Treatment. A Report to the President of the United States March. https://prescancerpanel.cancer.gov/report/drugvalue/pdf/PresCancerPanel_DrugValue_Mar2018.pdf

Price, M. (2012). Computational biologists: the next pharma scientists. Science Careers. Retrieved from http://www.sciencemag.org/careers/2012/04/computational-biologists-next-pharma-scientists.

Price AJ, Ndom P, Atenguena E, Mambou Nouemssi JP, Ryder RW(2012). Cancer care challenges in developing countries. Cancer. 2012;118:3627–3635. doi: 10.1002/cncr.26681

Prochaska J.O., Norcross J.C., Di Clemente C.C.(2013): Applying the stages of change. Psychother. Aust. 2013;19:10–15.

Public Health Foundation of India. (2011). A Critical Assessment of the Existing Health Insurance Models in India. A research study sponsored under the Scheme of Socio-Economic Research. New Delhi: The Planning Commission of India.

PUBLIC SECTOR RESEARCH FUNDING – OECD 2011, OECD Innovation Policy Platform, http://www.oecd.org/innovation/policyplatform/48136600.pdf

Quan, L. (2013). Pension coverage in China and the expansion of the new rural social pension. London: HelpAge International.

Quigley, F. (2015). Making Medicines Accessible: Alternatives to the Flawed Patent System. Retrieved from http://www.hhrjournal.org/2015/11/making-medicines-accessible-alternatives-to-the-flawed-patent-system-2/.

Ramsey, S., Blough, D., Kirchhoff, A., Kreizenbeck, K., Fedorenko, C., Snell, K., Newcomb, P., Hollingworth, W., Overstreet, K. (2013). Washington State cancer patients found to be at greater risk for bankruptcy than people without a cancer diagnosis. Health affairs (Project Hope), 32(6), 1143-52.

Rawson, N. (2012). Access to new oncology drugs in Canada compared with the United States and Europe. Fraser Institute. Retrieved from http://www.fraserinstitute.org/uploadedFiles/fraser-ca/Content/research-news/research/publications/access-to-new-oncology-drugs-in-canada.pdf.

Rawson, N. (2013). Potential impact of delayed access to five oncology drugs in Canada. Fraser Research Bulletin. Retrieved from http://www.fraserinstitute.org/uploadedFiles/fraser-ca/Content/research-news/research/publications/potential-impact-of-delayed-access-to-five-oncology-drugs-in-canada.pdf.

Reitsma, D., & Berry, S. (2013). Adaptive Trial Designs to Advance Oncology Research. Wilmington, NC: PPD.

Reuben, S., Milliken, E. L., & Paradis, L. J. (2012). The future of cancer research: accelerating scientific innovation. In President's Cancer Panel Annual Report 2010-2011. Washington: The President's Cancer Panel.

Reuter, S., Gupta, S. C., Chaturvedi, M. M., & Aggarwal, B. B. (2010). Oxidative stress, inflammation, and cancer: how are they linked?. *Free radical biology & medicine*, 49(11), 1603-16.

Rocchi, A., Menon, D., Verma, S., & Miller, E. (2008). The role of economic evidence in Canadian oncology reimbursement decision-making: to lambda and beyond. Value in Health. 11(4), 771–783.

Rx&D (2013). The R&D international report on access to medicines, 2011-2012. Canada's Research-Based Pharmaceutical Companies (Rx&D). Retrieved from http://www.canadapharma.org/CMFiles/Our%20Industry/Industry%20Facts/20130613_IRAM_2012_en_web.pdf.

Sanyal, A. & Singh, C. (2013). Universal pension scheme in India, IIM Bangalore research paper no. 420. Retrieved from http://ssrn.com/abstract=2310453.

Scannell, J.W., Blanckley, A., Boldon, H., & Warrington, B. (2012). Diagnosing the decline in pharmaceutical R&D efficiency. National Rev. Drug-Discovery 11, 191– 200. doi:10.1038/nrd3681.

Scheil-Adlung, X., & Sandner, L. (2011). Paid sick leave: incidence, patterns and expenditure in times of crises. SSRN Working Paper Series.

Scheil-Adlung, X. (2014). Universal health protection: progress to date and the way forward in social protection policy papers. Geneva, Switzerland: International Labour Organization.

Schnipper, L. E., & Bastian, A. (2016). New Frameworks to Assess Value of Cancer Care: Strengths and Limitations. The oncologist, 21(6), 654-8.

Siegel, R.L., Miller, K.D., Jemal, A.(2016) Cancer statistics, 2016. CA Cancer J Clin ; 66:7-30.

Shapiro, C. (2001). "Navigating the patent thicket: Cross–licenses, patent pools, and standard–setting." in Innovation Policy and the Economy ed. by Jaffe, A., J. Lerner, and S. Stern, NBER.

Shim, J. S., & Liu, J. O. (2014). Recent Advances in Drug Repositioning for the Discovery of New Anticancer Drugs. International Journal of Biological Sciences, 10(7), 654–663. http://doi.org/10.7150/ijbs.9224.

Simmen, F. A., & Simmen, R. C. (2011). The maternal womb: a novel target for cancer prevention in the era of the obesity pandemic?. European journal of cancer prevention : the official journal of the European Cancer Prevention Organisation (ECP), 20(6), 539-48.

Simoncelli, T. (2013). Paving the way for personalized medicine: FDA's role in a new era of medical product development. Silver Spring, Maryland: US Food and Drug Administration.

Smith, T.J., Hillner, B.E. Bending the cost curve in cancer care. New England Journal of Medicine 2011;364:2060–5.

Slavin, J. L., & Lloyd, B. (2012). Health benefits of fruits and vegetables. Advances in nutrition (Bethesda, Md.), 3(4), 506-16. doi:10.3945/an.112.002154

Soerjomataram, I., Lortet-Tieulent, J., Ferlay, J., Forman, D., Mathers, C., Parkin, D.M., Bray, F. (2012). Estimating and validating disability-adjusted life years at the global level: a methodological framework for cancer. BMC Med Res Methodol 2012, 12:125 doi: 10.1186/1471-2288-12-125.

Soliman, H., & Agresta, S. V. (2008). Current issues in adolescent and young adult cancer survivorship. Cancer control: Journal of the Moffitt Cancer Center. 15(1), 55–62.

Sood, N., Bendavid, E., Mukherji, A., Wagner, Z., Nagpal, S., Mullen P. (2014). Government health insurance for people below poverty line in India: quasi-experimental evaluation of insurance and health outcomes. BMJ. 349, g5114.

Steinmetz KA, Potter JD. Vegetables, fruit, and cancer prevention(1996): a review. Journal of the American Dietetic Association. 1996;96:1027–1039.

Stiglitz, J. E., & Jayadev, A. (2010). Medicine for tomorrow: some alternative proposals to promote socially beneficial research and development in pharmaceuticals. Journal of Generic Medicines: The Business Journal for the Generic Medicines Sector. 7(3), 217–226.

Sullivan, R., Peppercorn, J., Sikora, K., Zalcberg, J., Meropol, N. J., Amir, E., Khayat, D., Boyle, P., Autier, P., Tannock, I., Fojo, T., Siderov, J., Williamson, S., Camporesi, S., McVie, J. G., Purushotham, A. D., Naredi, P., Eggermont, A., Brennan, M. F., Steinberg, M. L., De Ridder, M., McCloskey, S. A., Verellen, D., Roberts, T., Storme, G., Hicks, R. J., Ell, P. J., Hirsch, B. R., Carbone, D. P., Schulman, K. A., Catchpole, P., Taylor, D., Geissler, J., Brinker, N. G., Meltzer, D., Kerr, D., &Aapro, M. (2011). Delivering affordable cancer care in high-income countries. The Lancet Oncology. 12(10), 933–980.

Sweitzer, S. J., Briley, M. E., Roberts-Gray, C., Hoelscher, D. M., Harrist, R. B., Staskel, D. M., & Almansour, F. D. (2010). Lunch is in the bag: increasing fruits, vegetables, and whole grains in sack lunches of preschool-aged children. Journal of the American Dietetic Association, 110(7), 1058-64.

Tassey, G. (2014). "Competing in Advanced Manufacturing: The Need for Improved Growth Models and Policies." The Journal of Economic Perspectives 28(1): 27-48.

Taylor, D. W. (2014a). Benefits outweigh costs in universal healthcare: business case for reimbursement of take-home cancer medicines in Ontario and Atlantic Canada. The American journal of the medical sciences. 4(4), 126–138.

Taylor, D. W. (2014b). The institutionalized discrimination of cancer patients—not what Tommy Douglas intended: a business case for the universal coverage of oral cancer medicines in Ontario and Atlantic Canada. Cambridge, Ontario. The Cameron Institute.

Tefferi, A., Kantarjian, H., Rajkumar, S. V., Baker, L. H., Abkowitz, J. L., Adamson, J. W., Bast, R.C. (2015). In support of a patient-driven initiative and petition to lower the high price of cancer drugs. Mayo Clinic Proceedings. 90(8), 996–1000.

Thomas, David. (2012). Oncology clinical trials—secrets of success. Retrieved from http://www.biotech-now.org/business-and-investments/2012/02/oncology-clinical-trials-secrets-of-success.

Tran G and Zafar S Yousuf (2018) Financial toxicity and implications for cancer care in the era of molecular and immune therapies. Annals of Translational Medicine, 6(9), 166, 2018

Trusheim, M. R., Berndt, E. R. & Douglas, F. L. (2007). Stratified medicine: strategic and economic implications of combining drugs and clinical biomarkers. Nature Reviews. Drug Discovery. 6, 287–293.

Tsimicalis, A. (2010). Costs incurred by families of children newly diagnosed with cancer in Ontario. Doctoral Theses, School of Graduate Studies, University of Toronto

Turner Associates & the Canadian Cancer Society. 2009. Cancer Drug Access for Canadians. Toronto: Canadian Cancer Society.

Uauy R., Solomons N(2005). Diet, nutrition, and the life-course approach to cancer prevention. J. Nutr. 2005;135:2934S–2945S.

Urberg KA, Değirmencioğlu SM, Pilgrim C(1997). Close friend and group influence on adolescent cigarette smoking and alcohol use. Dev Psychol. 1997;33(5):834

UN 2015: Transforming our world: the 2030 Agenda for Sustainable Development Department of Economics and Social Affairs. Disease Control Priorities, 3rd edition, DCP-3.

UN (2015 b): Department of Economic and Social Affairs, Population Division (2015). World Population Aging 2015 (ST/ESA/SER.A/390).

UNESCO(2017): What is the optimal balance between basic and applied research? Media Services, 16.02.2017 - Natural Sciences Sector, http://

www.unesco.org/new/en/media-services/single-view/news/what_is_the_optimal_balance_between_basic_and_applied_resear/

Vaudano, E. (2013). The innovative medicines initiative: A public private partnership model to foster drug discovery. Computational and Structural Biotechnology Journal. 6(7), 1–7.

Vineis P., Wild C.P. Global cancer patterns: Causes and prevention. Lancet. 2014;383:549–557. doi: 10.1016/S0140-6736(13)62224-2.

Vogelstein, B., Papadopoulos, N., Velculescu, V. E., Zhou, S., Diaz, L. A., &Kinzler, K. W. (2013). Cancer genome landscapes. Science 2013; 339: 1546-1558. Retrieved from http://www.ncbi.nlm.nih.gov/pmc/articles/PMC3749880/.

Vucic, E.A., Thu, K. L., Robison, K., Rybaczyk, L. A., Chari, R., Alvarez, C.E., & Lam, W. L. (2012). Translating cancer 'omics' to improved outcomes. Genome research. 22(2), 188–195.

White MC, Peipins LA, Watson M, Trivers KF, Holman DM, Rodriguez JL. Cancer prevention for the next generation. J Adolesc Health. 2013 May;52(5 Suppl):S1–7.

WHO(2011): Primary Prevention of Cancer Through mitigation of environmental and occupational determinants, International Conference, March 17, 18

WHO 2018, International Agency for Research on cancer, press release 12 September, 2018.

WHO 2006-2007: Cancer Control: Knowledge into Action: WHO Guide for Effective Programs: Modules 1-6.

WHO 2013: Arguing for Universal Health Coverage

World Health Organization. (2014). Global status report on non-communicable diseases. Retrieved from http://apps.who.int/iris/bitstream/10665/148114/1/9789241564854_eng.pdf?ua=1.

WHO(2018): Pricing of cancer medicines and its impacts. Technical Report

Wood JD, Richardson RI, Nute GR, Fisher AV, Campo MM, Kasapidou E, Sheard PR, Enser M(2003). Effects of fatty acids on meat quality: a review. Meat Sci. 2003;66:21–32.

Yakhini, Z., & Jurisica, I. (2011). Cancer computational biology.BioMed Central Bioinformatics. 12(1), 1–4.

Yang YT, Nagai S, Chen BK, Qureshi ZP, Lebby AA, Kessler S, et al. Generic oncology drugs: are they all safe? Lancet Oncol. 2016;17(11):e493–e501.

Yerramilli, P., & Jiang, X. X. (2013). Financing Cancer Care and Control in China. Harvard Global Equity Initiative. Retrieved from http://hgei.harvard.edu/fs/docs/icb.topic910623.files/DCP3%20Input%20-%20China.pdf.

Yu, H. (2015). Universal health insurance coverage for 1.3 billion people: what accounts for China's success? Health Policy. 119(9), 1145–52.

Williams H (2013): Intellectual property rights and innovation: Evidence from the human genome, Journal of Political Economy Vol. 121, No. 1 (February 2013), pp. 1-273

Woodcock J, Woosley R (2008) The FDA critical path initiative and its influence on new drug development. Annu Rev Med 59: 1–12.

Woodcock, J., Joseph, P., Griffin, J. D., & Behrman, R.E. (2011). Development of Novel Combination Therapies. N Engl J Med 2011; 364:985-987March 17, 2011DOI: 10.1056/ NEJMp1101548.

Yousuf ZS(2015). Financial toxicity of cancer care: It's time to intervene. J Natl Cancer Inst. 2015 ; 108 : djv370.

Zafar, S. Y., Peppercorn, J. M., Schrag, D., Taylor, D. H., Goetzinger, A. M., Zhong, X., & Abernethy, A. P. (2013). The financial toxicity of cancer treatment: a pilot study assessing out-of-pocket expenses and the insured cancer patient's experience. The oncologist, 18(4), 381–390. doi:10.1634/theoncologist.2012-0279

Zafar Y S (2016), Financial Toxicity of Cancer Care: It's Time to Intervene, JNCI: Journal of the National Cancer Institute, Volume 108, Issue 5, May 2016, djv370,

Zang, Y., & Lee, J. J. (2014). Adaptive clinical trial designs in oncology. Chinese Clinical Oncology, 3(4), 49. http://doi.org/10.3978/j.issn.2304-3865.2014.06.04.

Zehouni E A (2005) Translational and Clinical Science — Time for a New Vision, N Engl J Med 2005; 353:1621-1623.

Endnotes

1 The percentage of people who survive a certain type of cancer for a specific amount of time.

2 American Cancer Society, Facts & Figures 2018: Rate of Deaths From Cancer Continues Decline, Jan 4 2018. https://www.cancer.org/latest-news/facts-and-figures-2018-rate-of-deaths-from-cancer-continues-decline.html

3 The number of new cases occurring in a specified period and geographic area, conveyed either as an absolute number of cases per annum or as a rate per 100,000 persons per year is termed as incidence in epidemiology. Incidence data are produced by population-based cancer registries (PBCRs) (Bray et al 2018).

4 Age-standardized rates are used for comparison purpose, If the two populations being compared have different age distributions and the risk of the disease or outcome varies across the age groups. The computation of age-standardized rates requires the researcher to select an arbitrary standard population. For a numerical illustration see https://www.health.ny.gov/diseases/chronic/ageadj.htm

5 The estimate for DALYs lost due to cancer worldwide was 169 million years of healthy years lost in 2008 for 27 cancers and 184 countries (Soerjomataram et al 2012).

6 In the epidemiological field, a distinction is made between incidence and prevalence rates. Prevalence differs from incidence in that prevalence in-

cludes all cases, both new and preexisting, in the population at the specified time, whereas incidence is limited to new cases only.

7 GLOBOCAN project provides contemporary estimates of incidence of mortality and prevalence from major types of Cancer, at national level, for 184 countries of the world.

8 There are two kinds of prevalence: point prevalence and period prevalence. Point prevalence = (Number of current cases (new and preexisting) at a specified point in time/ Population at the same specified point in time Period Prevalence: (Number of current cases (new and preexisting) over a specified period of time/ Average or mid-interval population). In the above definitions, pre-exiting cases refer to survivors.

9 YLD is estimated by the years lived with disability, estimated as number of prevalent cases (P) multiplied by disability weight.

10 The following discussion draws upon WHO (2007): Prevention. (Cancer control: knowledge into action: WHO guide for effective programs; module 2.) WHO (2002) National cancer control programme: policies and managerial guidelines. – 2nd ed.

11 While our body needs oxidation for our immune system to work, for our body to protect itself through killing off old cells to make room for new ones, but oxidation turns oxidative stress when there's too much so that its products (free radicals) damage the DNA to cause malignant cells or inhibit the mechanism that can clear cancer cells from our body. Continued oxidative stress can lead to chronic inflammation (Reuter et al 2010). Free radicals and oxidants, thus, play a dual role as both toxic and beneficial compounds (Pham-Huy et al 2008).

12 These include proteins, carbohydrates, nucleic acids (DNA, RNA), and lipids

13 Alcohol and Cancer: A Statement of the American Society of Clinical Oncology Noelle K. LoConte, Abenaa M. Brewster, Judith S. Kaur, Janette K. Merrill, and Anthony J. Alberg 2018

14 Smoking and Drinking in America Today, Blog July 28, 2014,

15 A research study is a longitudinal study that follows over time groups of individuals who are alike in many ways but differ by a certain characteristic

(for example, female nurses who smoke and those who do not smoke) and compares them for a particular outcome (such as lung cancer) (The NCI Dictionary of Cancer Terms).

16 By definition, a case-control study is always retrospective because it starts with an outcome then traces back to investigate exposures (Lewallen et al 1998). Lewallen, S., & Courtright, P. (1998). Epidemiology in practice: case-control studies. Community eye health, 11(28), 57-8.

17 Prognostic studies are studies that examine selected predictive variables or risk factors and assess their influence on the outcome of a disease (Mak and Kum 2005).

18 Excessive reactive oxygen species (ROS) formation can induce oxidative stress, leading to cell damage that can culminate in cell death. Therefore, cells have antioxidant networks to scavenge excessively produced ROS (Poljsak, Šuput, & Milisav, 2013).

19 An in vitro (latin: "in the glass") test is a study that is performed outside of a living organism (i.e., glass, petri dishes). The test usually involves the use of isolated tissues, organs or cells. In contrast, an in vivo (latin: "in the living") test is a study that is performed in living organisms (i.e., rat, rabbit). More precisely, while in vitro testing generally involves the use of test systems such as isolated organs, tissues or cell cultures, in vivo testing involves live models (NAMSA).

20 https://www.who.int/features/qa/cancer-red-meat/en/

21 http://www.aicr.org/reduce-your-cancer-risk/diet/red-and-processed-meat.html

22 The VIP value is a weighted sum of squares of the PLS weights ( ), which takes into account the explained variance of each PLS dimension. Notationally, $VIP_j = \sqrt{\frac{p}{\Sigma SS(b_m t_m)} \Sigma \omega_{mj}^2 SS(b_m t_m)}$, where p is the number of variables, M(the superscript over ∑) the number of retained latent variables, ωmj the PLS weight of the j-th variable for the m-th latent variable and SS(bmtm) is the percentage change of the dependent variable explained by the m-th latent variable.

23 Statnotes, from North Carolina State University https://pdfs.semanticscholar.org/a0fd/a257a074239d70c342f25b2d39668d7b5f20.pdf

[24] PLS is based on the singular value decomposition of *X 'Y*.

[25] The Panel describes term financial toxicity, as the negative impact of cancer care costs on patients and their families and caregivers.

[26] The market is considered highly concentrated in certain cancer therapeutic areas. For example, three companies – Bristol-Myers Squibb, Ono Pharmaceutical and Merck & Co – accounted for nearly 97% of the 2017 global market for the melanoma medicines (WHO 2018).

[27] USA Today/Kaiser Family Foundation/Harvard School of Public Health. National Survey of Households Affected by Cancer. November 2006.

[28] There is no standard definition of a "me-too" drug. Hollis (2004) defines Me-too drugs as products which largely duplicate the action of existing drugs.

[29] This para heavily draws upon Danzon and Taylor (2010). For more elaborate discussion, see the section on Value based pricing.

[30] The following draws upon page 190 in American Society of Clinical Oncology (2018): American Society of Clinical Oncology Position Statement on Addressing the Affordability of Cancer Drugs ASCO Special Article, Journal of Oncology Practice, Volume 14 / Issue 3 / March 2018

[31] Which are products isolated from living organisms or systems (The President's Cancer Panel, 2018)

[32] A biosimilar product is a biologic product that is created in living cells and is approved based on demonstrating that it is highly similar to an FDA approved biologic product, known as a reference product, and has no clinically meaningful differences in terms of safety and effectiveness from the reference product. Only minor differences in clinically inactive components are allowable in biosimilar products.

[33] When the outcome is unknown, Kremer recommends an incentive system like "patent buy-outs"

[34] To spur pharmaceutical drug innovation, modern research suggests two mechanisms, (i) "push" programs (public subsidies of biomedical research and clinical trials) and "pull" programs (impact-based and royalty-based rewards for new drugs). Lum-sum rewards come under "pull programs" (Grootendorst et al (2011)

[35] Typically, R&D productivity is measured as the ratio of R&D output to inputs.

[36] New Drug Application (NDA) and Biologic License Application (BLA) approvals.

[37] The following model is reproduced from Paul et al., 2010).

[38] American Association for Cancer Research(AACR) 2018 Harnessing Research discoveries for Patient Benefit. " Basket trials test one given therapeutic on a group of patients who all have the same type of genetic mutation, regardless of the anatomic site of the original cancer." "Umbrella trials test multiple therapeutics across multiple genetic mutations on a group of patients, all of whom have cancer arising in the same anatomic site"(AACR 2018 P50). See

[39] Trials that enroll patients based on a genomic alteration rather than a disease type are basket trials. "Umbrella" trials (BATTLE, I-SPY) refer to trials examining one tumor type with multiple drugs and predictive biomarkers

[40] In 'Basket Trials'- single treatment and single biomarker, different histologies placed in baskets. In Umbrella trials-single histology-multiple biomarkers each matched to treatments

[41] See equation (i) above or 'pharmaceutical value equation' (i), in Paul et al (2010).

[42] A surrogate endpoint as is defined as a biomarker intended to substitute for a clinical endpoint (Cohn, 2004).

[43] Under the commons model, the federal government sponsored pre-marketer "upstream" research and encouraged broad dissemination of results in the public domain. Unpatented biomedical discoveries were freely incorporated in "downstream" products for diagnosing and treating disease (Heller &Eisenberg, 1998, p 698).

[44] Human Genome Project, a publicly-funded project to map the human genome, for future use in medical testing and medicine.

[45] The Translational Research Working Group defined a translational continuum and developed a "roadmap" to create a stronger research infrastructure to accelerate the clinical research enterprise. To see the steps involved along the translational pathway, refer to Cancer Information &

Support Network (2006).

46 http://cbioportal.org

47 measured in petabytes, where a petabyte is a million billion bytes

48 As per World Bank's classification, low and middle-income countries are countries with per capita income (in 2005) falling in the following range: low income, US$875 or less; lower middle income, US$876–3,465; upper middle income, and US$3,466–10,725. High income countries are those that have per capita income above US$10,725.

49 Brady, Fullerton, and Cross's 2010 cross-national study on working poverty in high-income countries defines a household as working poor if 1) it has at least one employed person and 2) the total household income falls below 50% of the median income for that country.

50 Out-of-pocket costs for cancer c include health insurance deductibles, co-insurance, and co-payments for covered services, as well as services that are not covered by insurance (IOM(Institute of Medicine), 2014).

51 The reforms under this leg include outlawing exclusions for pre-existing conditions and other discriminatory practices, guaranteeing access to non-group insurance and imposing limits on the ability of insurers to charge differential prices by health status—prices for a given product can only vary by age and smoking status. In addition, minimum standards are set for insurance in the non-group and small group markets, including a list of 'essential benefits' that must be included in an insurance package, and a minimum 'actuarial value' (the share of total spending on the essential benefits package that is covered, on average for a typical population, by insurance) (Gruber, 2011).

52 A situation characterized as a 'free ride' refers to a person remaining uninsured until they are sick and then buying insurance at average prices.

53 As Gruber has mentioned, most uninsured are not the poorest Americans, but the 'working poor'—those whose income and age leaves them ineligible for public insurance coverage, and who are not offered insurance through their places of employment (Gruber, 2011). The only avenue available to such individuals is the non-group insurance market (Gruber, 2008).

54 Canadian Institute for Health Information

55 After treatment and during palliative and terminal care, there is also a possibility of early retirement (Sullivan et al., 2011).

56 The non-salaried population includes self-employed workers, the under-employed, the unemployed, and people out of the labor market permanently or temporarily, along with their families.

57 In-work poverty is often related to insufficient work participation, resulting from very short part-time work or very short employment spells over the year. In a number of countries, disposable income of couples with children does not exceed 60% of the median income when both spouses are working full-time in low-paid employment.

58 Doha Declaration of TRIPS Agreement.

59 Affordability in the research literature is estimated as drug prices divided by GDP per capita or average salary (Gyawali B. (2017)

60 External Reference Pricing (ERP) is the system by which a country health authority uses the price information from other countries when negotiating prices with a pharmaceutical company. Like parallel trade, ERP tends to reduce price differentials between countries.

61 Trade-Related Aspects of Intellectual Property Rights.

62 ILO report (2017) has described eight options that are available to governments to generate additional resources for social protection. Some of these options include: re-allocating public expenditures from low-impact investments with those with larger socio-economic impacts; increasing tax revenue by strengthening the efficiency of tax collection methods and overall compliance; expanding social security coverage and contributory revenues; and adopting a more accommodating macroeconomic framework- even if this entails allowing for higher budget deficit paths and/or higher levels of inflation without jeopardizing macroeconomic stability.

63 Brazil, Russian Federation, India, China and South Africa.

64 Incidence refers to new cases that develop in a given period of time, while prevalence refers to the number of cases of a disease that are present in a particular population at a given time. Prevalence = (Incidence Rate) x (Average Duration of Disease)

65 WHO (2002): National cancer control programme: policies and manag-

erial guidelines. – 2nd ed.

66 Authoritarian parenting, also called strict parenting, with little open dialogue between parent and child. Permissive parenting, on the other hand, is style of parenting in which parents tend to be lenient while trying to avoid confrontation.

67 https://www.cancer.org/treatment/treatments-and-side-effects/treatment-types/immunotherapy/cancer-vaccines.html

68 GICR is a multi-partner response to the disparity in robust cancer statistics across the globe, led by the International Agency for Research on Cancer (IARC) and Union for International Cancer Control (UICC).

69 Non-communicable disease.

Made in United States
Orlando, FL
04 November 2026

90205467R00088